friendship, help and encouragement. Best wishes, Armando

MENDING CHILDREN'S BROKEN HEARTS

Musings Based on Conversations, Observations and
Notes by My Spouse Grace S. Wolff, M.D.

by ARMANDO I. PEREZ, PH.D.
JANUARY 2017

DORRANCE
PUBLISHING CO
EST. 1920
PITTSBURGH, PENNSYLVANIA 15238

The contents of this work, including, but not limited to, the accuracy of events, people, and places depicted; opinions expressed; permission to use previously published materials included; and any advice given or actions advocated are solely the responsibility of the author, who assumes all liability for said work and indemnifies the publisher against any claims stemming from publication of the work.

Dorrance Publishing Co
585 Alpha Drive
Suite 103
Pittsburgh, PA 15238
Visit our website at *www.dorrancebookstore.com*

ISBN: 978-1-4809-4345-2
eISBN: 978-1-4809-4322-3

DEDICATION

This book is dedicated to the universal family of caregivers, departed and living, from the medical field and from all walks of life.

TABLE OF CONTENTS

FOREWORD

My beloved wife Grace S. Wolff, M.D., a devoted Pediatric Cardiologist, died on July 16, 2015 of the neurological disease known as ALS (Lou Gehrig's disease). I feel privileged to have been her life companion. ALS is a very challenging disease, especially for a physician who knows exactly what is happening and what is to come. I am grateful to caregivers in Florida (the ALS Center at the University of Miami's Neurology Department and other local support staff), and caregivers in New York State during a farewell vacation there, for taking very good care of Grace.

I wanted to make a record of my late wife's loving concern with the emotional as well as medical needs of children and their parents, shown while facing life and death situations. During our long time together she related many stories, wrote some notes, and shared with me interactions as she continued to care for her "extended family" of patients. Much of the written material was done in the early phase of her career, prior to her moving from New York State to Florida in 1977; I believe the content is still relevant, especially from an emotional standpoint. As a tribute to her I wanted to share these thoughts with others; to write down some of the stories behind those smiling snapshots which graced our refrigerator/bulletin board, in the hopes that her insights might bring about reduced anxiety and suffering.

First, a few words about Grace. She was born in Rome, NY, a late and unexpected child of blue-collar parents, both devout Catholics. She attended the Academy of the Holy Names, where she told the nuns she wanted to become a priest. The nuns explained that women could not become priests, so at age eleven she decided that she would become a medical doctor instead: she could care for her disease-prone parents and others with limited means. Upon graduation from high school she worked as a secretary and nurse apprentice in a medical office, to earn money for her education at LeMoyne College in Syracuse, NY. Then she attended medical school at Marquette University (now Medical College of Wisconsin). After graduation she trained at Columbia Presbyterian Hospital in New York City and at Harvard University's Boston Children's Hospital. This training led to her distinguished career as an innovative Pediatric Cardiologist, introducing catheters into children's hearts for diagnostic purposes and treatments. At the University of Miami Medical School she trained scores of physicians now practicing in the U.S. and abroad. In spite of her many scientific achievements, she is best remembered, perhaps, by her warmth and sensitivity toward her small patients and their parents, always taking the time to understand the total medical and familial picture.

Based on her patients' parents' comments over the course of her career, Grace felt that, in general, parents sufficiently understood the scientific and technical aspects of procedures and surgeries to which their patients were subjected. On the other hand, parents and children had psychological needs which were often unmet. Sometimes parents felt guilty that they may have transmitted a genetic defect to their child. Others were unprepared for a child's rejection of them, and blame, for putting him/her through pain and discomfort.

Woven throughout this book is Grace's deep feeling of appreciation for the value of life, no matter how difficult, precarious or short it might be. Grace shares the joys of restoring a child to a fully healthy and normal life. She also shares the sadness for losses that occasionally happen, but with a comforting view that love between a lost child and his or her parents and caregivers will always remain.

In reworking Grace's unfinished material, I have taken some license, yet all the while carefully relying on my intimate knowledge of her feelings and character. To protect parents' and patients' privacy I have changed actual names, and altered or omitted immaterial facts. The only exception is the Testimonial at the beginning of the book, in which the actual name of the patient who authored it, Frank Conklin, is used, with his consent. His story is not otherwise featured in any of the chapters.

As noted earlier, the stories occurred mostly in the early years of Grace's career, i.e., in the early years of pediatric cardiac surgery. References in the stories about delaying surgery were based on limitations then in effect, such as those in heart-lung machines for infants. Further, the stories make little reference to the use of echocardiograms in diagnosis, which nowadays has decreased the need for invasive catheterizations for infants. In my view, the timeframe of the stories does not diminish the value of the message of hope for facing real crises with faith and courage.

Besides honoring Grace, I hope this book will provide some useful perspectives to physicians and parents caring for children, perhaps the most vulnerable of patients. I also hope that my wife's words will help caregivers with the emotional challenges of their demanding work, and in coping with devastating losses. Such was my case with Grace.

Armando I. Perez, Ph.D.

TESTIMONIAL TO DR. GRACE
MY SECOND MOTHER

There are two special women in my life. My mother gave birth to me. Dr. Grace gave me life. She is my second mother.

My name is Frank Conklin. I was born on June 9, 1971, in Glens Falls, New York, the child of Carol and George Conklin.

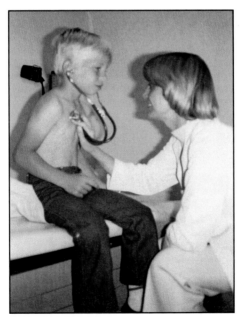

Grace makes child patient Frank relax by listening to his own heart.

I was born with a serious heart condition called aortic stenosis. When I became three years of age my mother explained to me: "Your heart is broken. The doctor is going to fix your broken heart." I had successful open heart surgery at Albany Medical Center in New York. To my knowledge it was the first open heart surgery in the new suite of the hospital. My case was featured in the hospital's annual report. Dr. Grace lovingly managed my care.

In 1974 my family and I moved to Florida, mostly because the weather here is more suitable for my health. Providentially, Dr. Grace moved to Florida also, to join the University of Miami Medical School faculty. She continued to be my doctor over the many years of checkups, phone consultations, birthday cards and Christmas cards. She held my hand and navigated me through the many turns of my care, including a heart valve replacement surgery at age sixteen.

Grace with patient Frank, now a strong adult who volunteers as a fireman.

Whenever she closed the door of the examination room, she gave me her undivided attention. I always had the feeling that I was her only patient. On the day of her retirement party, there was a roomful of people who expressed the same feeling. After her retirement, I continued to go to the University of Miami, to be cared for by her trusted colleagues.

I am now 45 years old. I enjoy living a healthy lifestyle. I have been a successful electrician for 24 years. Thanks to my improved health I have been able to care for my aging mother (recently deceased) and father. I also serve as a volunteer in the Key Largo, Florida Volunteer Fire and Rescue team. I felt a calling for this service because I wanted to help save other people's lives, just like Dr. Grace saved mine.

I feel that, to me and to the many others whom she gently touched, Dr. Grace's life is aptly described by the words in the popular song by Gladys Knight and the Pips: "You are the best thing that ever happened to me!" May her life continue to serve as an inspiration to me and to others!

Patient Frank (president of his local volunteer fire department)
in front of a retired fire truck he bought as his personal vehicle.

PART I
AFFIRMATION OF LIFE:
THE CHILD AND CAREGIVING HEROES

CHAPTER 1

Introduction: The Child As An Embodiment Of Life's Force

The child is all of life: the past, the present and the future. The child is the continuity of humankind; the previous generation is present and the future generation is promised in the child, who lives the present. All in the child is active, existing, and becoming. All senses are tuned to the universe. All must be seen, heard, smelled, tasted, and touched. All things must be united in that little self. Nothing escapes, for all of life must be captured. The child is the driving force, the open door to growth and happiness. The child lives fully and provides us with a greater understanding of life.

Each day there is so much for adults to see and learn. I perceive a greater understanding of life when I see a child who lives fully despite handicaps, and when I see the same child live even more fully when surgery has removed that handicap.

Most of all I understand life when I care for children who are close to death. They open my eyes to life's richness. These children show me the value of little things, the greatness of each breath, the ease of movement in and out, and the vitality of a strong heartbeat. These children teach me to cherish every word I say and hear, and to love all that I see. I love the blue sky of morning, the sunshine, the black sky of night, and the stars. I love the hands that can touch, that feel the coldness of snow, the warmth of another's face.

Children who are dying beg us to live intensely, to love the crisp smell of winter, the apple blossoms and lilacs of spring, the roses of summer and leaves of fall, to grasp, to know all of life. I know tranquility in the seasons' movements, my effortless harmony with all that is. So much to see and feel, the feeling is so deep it strikes the roots of my being.

My story tells about children who were born with heart disease. I write about the triumphs, the ones who had successful surgeries or procedures and are still with us. I also write about the losses and the intensity of feeling that they generated, for a critically ill or dying child is one of the most powerful forces uniting us as a true family of man. No sick children are ever alone; firm bonds are established with all who know them. When visiting a children's hospital, this unifying force is apparent. Children are concerned with one another; parents are involved with their own as well as others' children; medical personnel share themselves as well as their clinical expertise. There are many forgotten workers in hospitals who are also intimately involved with the children: laboratory technicians, volunteers, kitchen staff, and janitors. I have watched the pained faces of these concerned individuals hovering over a child that could not be cured: they share the devastation of losing a child, as well as the exhilaration of seeing successes.

But no one knows the depth of emotions as much as the parent of a critically ill child. Only parents know the depth of anxiety, fear, despair, frustration and anger; as well as the peace, confidence, hope, and love resulting from improvement or cure. In my story I include contributions from a few of these parents of critically ill children, parents of different social, educational, cultural and economic backgrounds. They provide a unifying message, a message that we are all one family. We share the love of life and the great appreciation of its value.

CHAPTER 2

Sung Heroes: The Medical Professionals

Those who customarily receive recognition for their achievements I call "Sung Heroes". In this category fall surgeons, medical specialists and nurses. It is distressing that, sometimes, bad publicity seems to overshadow good publicity about their work. Unfortunately, headlines frequently reflect bad results or bad behavior, and the good side is either not commented upon or is quickly forgotten. Fortunately, most of these professionals enjoy their work and find it very self-satisfying. Consequently, they do not need the recognition of the public. Still, recognition is gratifying. But the most magnificent gratification of all arises from seeing a sick child become well, and particularly, watching an oxygen-deprived "blue" child become pink, and go on to live a most marvelous life that this transformation granted. It is like watching a baby bird when it first learns to fly, or seeing a caterpillar metamorphose into a butterfly.

Surgeons carry an undeserved image of being detached from the patient. Some people have even suggested that this detachment is necessary for providing proper care, their rationale being that a surgeon involved with the patient is unable to make good judgments. Another rationale put forth is that such involvement might cause the surgeon to "freeze" in an emergency situation. My observation is that there are as many personality differences among surgeons as there are among people in general. I think it is a misconception that one needs to be detached from the patient to deliver good care. On the contrary, since medicine deals with human beings, its practice is as much of a human art as a science. I contend that better care is delivered when the physician is involved.

Let me return to the misconception that surgeons are generally detached from their patients. I have had the opportunity to know many surgeons, most of whom have been quite involved with their patients. Perhaps dealing with children, rather than with adults, elicits a greater involvement. Further, most of the surgeons I have known had children of their own, and I think that probably this circumstance resulted in a greater identity with patients.

Since my story concerns heart surgeons specifically, I must comment about some of them. I recall one who spent extra time with a little boy who was about to undergo the repair of a hole in his heart. The surgeon talked at length with the little boy and allayed his concerns, by establishing a shared identification with him, by pointing out that both of them had the same middle name. The surgeon discussed at length his successes as a medical evacuation officer on the Normandy beaches during World War II (the boy was well acquainted with literature on the war) and convinced the boy that his life was as important, or more so, than the life of any of the wounded soldiers.

I recall another surgeon who was extremely distressed that a little foster child would not be allowed to stay with his foster parents whom he so dearly loved.

The importance of emotional involvement notwithstanding, it is sometimes possible, and desirable, for the physician to temporarily turn off this involvement. All physicians do so occasionally, and some more than others. Sometimes we need to build an emotional wall to protect ourselves and recover our strength. For sometimes the stress is all-consuming. These are the times when we must gain perspective, to take a moment to see the green of grass, the blue of sky, the exhilaration of sunrise, and the serenity of a sunset. Also these are times to listen to the beautiful sounds of children laughing. Sometimes it is necessary for physicians to immerse themselves in the world of the well. Our sense of life is heightened. We are then ready to return to those who are sick.

CHAPTER 3

Unsung Heroes: Hospital Workers, Volunteers And Family Caregivers

Hospital Workers

Everyone knows about the surgeon and the other physicians involved in a child's care. Few know about the "unsung heroes" who take the child to themselves; for a child elicits love from all who surround him or her.

I have watched Jane, the kitchen aide, visit children in the Intensive Care Unit to find out their special food preferences (always verifying that they are within the doctor's orders) and otherwise doing special little favors for them. I have heard her inquire, time and time again, about the condition of a particular sick child.

Then there is another person behind the scenes whom one would think was uninvolved: the lady janitor. She has seen the respirator and the other machinery surrounding the child. But most of all she notices the child herself. The janitor mops the floor quietly, but her quietness speaks of her absorption with this little child, and of her concern. She says nothing, but she watches. She goes into the room after there has been difficulty, to clean up the spilled bottles and to pick up containers dropped on the floor because of the haste and urgency of a critical moment. She does not know the technicalities. She does not know the names of the drugs. She does not know the kidneys are functioning poorly. But she knows, with her human intuition, that the child is in danger. I recall one of the lady janitors stopping me in the parking lot saying:

"How is little Janice?" She was an interested, concerned human being who hurt for this child and was deeply moved and deeply involved.

There are so many others, such as Alice. Alice is a practical nurse and laboratory technician who has committed herself to the care of infants and children. It is not just a job. Alice becomes so involved with the children that sometimes her own health is in jeopardy, because her emotional commitment becomes an unbearable burden. This is particularly true when she is involved in the care of critically ill children for whom the death rate is high—children with leukemia, heart disease or kidney disease. But Alice's job is not just a nine-to-five. Yes, she works her eight hours a day, but the number of times that she does little "favors" is countless. She has been available for the child who has had heart surgery, from whom it is difficult to obtain a blood sample or to start an intravenous infusion. She has been available for the child who, after surgery, needs blood studies. Her expertise is in some situations greater than that of the nurses or physicians, and she makes herself available to the children. Another unsung hero.

Volunteers

The word "volunteer" conjures up many images, but rarely do images do justice to the full human commitment that one sees in volunteer workers involved with children and their parents.

I especially remember the anguished father of a newborn baby, who was waiting for his son to return from the operating room. Imagine the intensity of his emotion, knowing that his son had a 25-percent chance of dying at surgery. Besides, his wife was at another hospital recovering from her delivery. Fortunately, there was a volunteer there to comfort him.

Physicians and nurses make every effort to provide comfort, but because they must concentrate on their work, having a lay person to help is very valuable. It is true that there is little tangible to offer in trying times, but solace, coffee, and a comfortable waiting room are important to a worried family member. Often, volunteers facilitate communications between a waiting relative and the operating room.

A word about foster grandmothers: it is heart-warming to watch a foster grandmother and child together as the child is being comforted and caressed. That caress is even more powerful when seen amidst the sterility of the hospital environment. It is as though a protective aura surrounds the twosome. These wonderful ladies give their entire day to love a little one.

There is sometimes a mistaken impression that volunteer workers are well-to-do men and women who have nothing else to keep them busy. The perception is far from true. Most volunteers are very committed people from all walks of life, performing an indispensable service. They fill a void left by medical professionals who by necessity must attend to the technological aspects of care.

PART II
SUCCESS STORIES
AND LESSONS LEARNED

CHAPTER 4

Triumph After A Stormy Course

I remember Kristen. She is six now and I am looking at the picture her mother sent me, in which she stands with her sister waiting for the school bus. She is going to kindergarten. Her mother writes: "…you fought for her all the way, and let's face it, it was an awfully hard fight but worth it…I also realize she has a rough road ahead. If you could only see her when she is well! She loves everyone and everyone loves her. As different people have told me, she enjoys life and little things so much more than a normal child."

I can see little Kristen in my mind's eye on the day I first met her. She was a newborn baby and so very blue. Her serious heart defect, a three-chambered heart, was confirmed at cardiac catheterization. Surgery was performed immediately, but her course was very stormy. Even her first two years of life were stormy. She had heart failure and many respiratory infections. But she hung tenaciously to her life.

The wonderful pediatrician in Kristen's hometown was marvelous, and provided constant care for her and her parents. He continues to care for her and he, too, has shared in the gift of her life, for he has played such a large part. Kristen loves him; I am sure she knows she is here because of his help and care. I thank Kristen and her mom for sharing their good times with me. Meantime, darling Kristen is happy, knowing that her three-chambered heart is not normal, although living life as it were.

CHAPTER 5

Precarious Survival Against All Odds

Yesterday I received a picture of Mary. She is one year old now, too young to realize the miracle of her existence. I think of a year ago, when she arrived shortly after being in shock from congestive heart failure and septicemia (blood infection). She had no blood pressure and very weak pulses. The pulses in her legs were not present at all. This absence was a sign of coarctation of the aorta (a narrowing which obstructs blood flow in the main blood vessel of the body to the legs).

Despite her extreme condition, she was taken for cardiac catheterization to confirm the diagnosis. The diagnosis was indeed confirmed, but there was something more: she had a hole between the pumping chambers of the heart, and she had an obstructive mitral valve, the valve that allows blood to pass into the pumping chamber to the body.

The surgeon relieved the obstruction in the aorta, but he found it was too risky to try to repair the entire heart in her critically ill condition. She required medication to support her blood pressure. She became deficient in blood-clotting factors, a problem which sometimes accompanies severe infections and shock. Her septicemia resulted in an infection in her knee joint which required a cast.

Mary continued to hold onto life for many days, despite one complication after another. Not a single physician predicted that she would survive. Yet she began to improve, and some days later went home.

For Mary's parents, her history was a process of birth-death-rebirth, for because of our warnings they had been prepared for the inevitability of her death. Then they were presented with the "unreality" of her life. I can only imagine the emotional and psychological maneuvers that her parents must have undertaken to deal with the contradictions at hand. In any case, I deeply realize the specialness of this little child.

I see that specialness each time that I see Mary and her mother. Surely her parents worry about the future. What will her next catheterization show? Will she survive her next surgery? Will she be normal mentally, after having suffered so many complications? Such is the burden on these parents, and yet there is such a joy that counters that burden!

Mary's mom writes: "There are many times I wish you could be with us to see the many things and expressions she goes through. She has learned total control of her bouncing and will turn around and around, twirling herself silly. Some months ago I bought a baby seat for my bicycle and for the last week we have been biking for an hour every day. Mary stretches her hands up as high as she can to catch the wind and hums to herself...There is not a day of my life that goes by without positive and happy thoughts...seeing a special little girl that your expertise and love help to preserve...I feel that same joy and delight in her existence and I love life more because of her."

How generous and sensitive for the mother to share so much with me!

CHAPTER 6

A Risky Surgery Succeeds After Many Worries

Charlie's surgery is scheduled. It is no longer a future event that can be postponed. It is now—the present. There are only a few weeks to wait. It can no longer be denied. The mother cries as she looks at her child at play. Following are the mother's thoughts, then Grace's:

Mother's Thoughts:
What anxiety in that anticipation! The mother asks: "Will he live? They told me the risk of dying is small, but that seems not so small when it is the life of my child! My neighbor's baby died at surgery and his risk was low too. Will my child suffer? Will he feel pain? Will he understand why he hurts? Will he be frightened in the Intensive Care Unit, with all the machinery and the strange sounds with all the doctors and nurses that he does not know? Will I be able to be with him? Will he blame me for allowing this to happen to him? Is it my fault that he has a heart problem at all? Am I to blame for this whole thing? I am his mother…did I do something wrong when I was pregnant? I took an occasional aspirin…I had my teeth X-rayed (though I used an abdominal shield)…"

Grace's Thoughts:
So many thoughts and so many feelings occur within a single moment! I can answer questions. I can give reassurances, but the fears and anxieties will persist

unrelentingly until the surgery is accomplished and the living child rests again in the mother's arms. Facing the known is never as fearful as facing the unknown. To help parents gain a better understanding of medical and psychological issues, I am digressing from Charlie's story for a few paragraphs below, in which I summarize the information that over the years I have provided to parents such as Charlie's.

Grace's Generic Summary of Heart Defects, Surgeries and Impacts:
The risk of dying varies with each defect, but the more common heart defects carry a very low risk. The common defects are ventricular septal defects (hole in the wall between the lower heart chambers—the pumping chambers), atrial septal defect (hole in the wall between the upper chambers—the receiving chambers), persistent patent ductus arteriosus (a communication between the two main blood vessels that leave the heart), and pulmonary stenosis (narrowing of the valve that leads to the main blood vessel of the lung).

There are other defects which carry a higher risk. These are those that cause cyanosis (blueness). Some of the very complex defects are fraught with difficulties for repair. But the repair of the most common causes of blue heart disease, Tetralogy of Fallot and transposition of the two main blood vessels arising from the heart, can generally be performed with a reasonably low risk, except for the unusual forms of these defects. Usually the differences between the usual and unusual forms of these defects are apparent after careful study by cardiac catheterization and echocardiogram (a means to view the heart using ultrasound). These differences between the usual and unusual forms affect the risk figures. Parents may read an article that quotes a seven-percent risk for Tetralogy of Fallot and wonder why their doctor quoted fifteen percent for their own child; most likely the discrepancy is due to the severity of this particular form of Tetralogy, or the presence of other associated defects.

Because of the different gradations of severity, which are difficult to quantify exactly by tests, there is an element of judgment and subjectivity in the estimation of risk factors and even in the determination of the best treatment. Often it is wise to get second opinions. Fortunately, most physicians welcome other opinions, and if a parent desires another consultant, arrangements can be made easily. In fact, in the most difficult cases, the patient's cardiologist may of his/her own initiative send the patient's data (X-rays, electrocardiograms, and angiograms—pictures of the heart taken during catheterization) to one or more other major medical centers. There is a camaraderie in the field of Pediatric Cardiology which allows for free exchange and mutual assistance.

Regarding a parent's fear of pain, the truth is that despite the many analgesic agents for pain relief, there is still a certain amount of discomfort that will accompany open-heart surgery. Of course, the surgery itself will be performed under total anesthesia. However, there will be a certain amount of pain during the post-operative period, even though strong analgesic medications are used. But surgery carries more than physical pain...it carries a powerful psychological impact. The small child cannot understand the pain, the unfamiliar environment and faces, and the absence of his constant companions—his mother and father.

Frequently, immediately after surgery the child will turn away from his parents when they visit. He holds them responsible for what has happened. But typically in a few days he "forgives" them and appears not to have suffered a lasting insult. I recall a three-month old baby who would not smile at his parents for a week after his cardiac catheterization. At the age of five he had heart surgery and reacted similarly. Very much later, after the surgery, he had been at home for some time when his mother said to him, "Jimmy, it wasn't too bad, was it?" And he replied, "I felt real bad on the inside."

There is much that is being done to help these little people through their trying time. Visiting hours in ICUs have been liberalized and parents are encouraged to be with their children as much as possible. When the child leaves the ICU, it is very advisable for the parents to room-in, to reassure the child and themselves. Also, playroom facilities and teachers provide a pleasant environment and distract from the unpleasantness of the hospital experience.

Charlie's Day 1 Post-Operative: Looking Pink Again
Back to Charlie's story...he is now ten hours post-operative. Great news! His blood pressure is normal; his heart rate is normal. He looks like a little mechanical man with so many attachments for his respiration—the cardiac monitor, the arterial line, the pacemaker and tubes everywhere—chest, blood vessels, nose, mouth, and penis. Despite all of that, he is beautiful! He is an eleven-month old baby who survived a long operation on the heart-lung machine, a risky operation with a twenty-percent chance of dying. Before surgery

he was so blue—his lips like dark plums—now he is rosy red. What a marvel! Life is so precious when death is so close. His life will be so much better, free of constant fatigue!

There is a thermometer which constantly records Charlie's temperature. During surgery his temperature was lowered to reduce the risk. This is typically done by means of circulatory blood which has been cooled in the pump (heart-lung machine). I had watched Charlie's temperature gradually fall from the normal 37 degrees C to 28 degrees. The EKG showed a decreasing heart rate from 120 beats per minute to 20, and then to a horizontal line (no beats). The EEG (brain wave recording) also showed a gradual decrease.

Charlie's heart had been bathed in an iced solution to induce "cold cardiplegia" (a cold-paralyzed heart); it had been flaccid and unresisting as its reconstruction was undertaken. The Dacron fabric had been custom-cut and stitched into place, while the blood was rerouted for oxygenation to correct nature's deficiency. Technically everything looked good…but the real test came when his heart was asked to function in its reconstructed state. Fortunately, after the key words "let's warm him" were said, and the blood in the pump was heated slowly, the brain waves could be seen again. The heart emitted first one beep, and then more. The heart rate had risen slowly to the regular 120 beats per minute. The flaccid heart muscle had recovered its resilience and had contracted forcefully. Charlie was back again and healthier.

But there was one more step before we could relax. Would his heart function when disconnected from the heart-lung machine? For twenty minutes all had been well…and then his heart rate had dropped to 40. The blood pressure came down. We had given a medication…small improvement. Then we gave a higher dose…all was well. It had been a brief, frightening moment, but we had managed to give the correct medication and his heart was pleased for it.

Now Charlie is in the Heart Recovery Room. I keep looking at him—a beautiful rose. He does not move for his muscles are paralyzed by the medicines used for anesthesia. It will be one or two more hours before he moves. I want to see him awake. I want to be sure that my celebration is not premature. Finally, I touch his pink little toes and he withdraws his foot—he is feeling and moving. What joy!

His mom and dad are worn. The day has been an eternity! They have been waiting for hours. They have been given progress reports during the surgery that everything was going well, but they must see him to really believe. Mom cries tears of joy, relief, triumph…and we cry with her!

The young couple approach the little one's bedside—a little haltingly—a little fearfully—but so filled with joy. Their baby lives.

Day 2: Great Post-Operative Condition

The critical 24-hour post-operative period is over. We removed the breathing tube and Charlie is breathing by himself with oxygen delivered by a mask. We gave him a little water and he took it ravenously. Tomorrow he will start on his regular liquids. In seven more days he will go home, no longer blue, no longer breathless, no longer fatigued by minimal exercise. He will go home with a stronger heart and a new life!

Days 3 and 4: Deterioration (Fluid Buildup)

I have not had time to write because I was too busy with the deterioration in Charlie's condition (fluid buildup).

Day 5: Improvement

Over the previous two days, there had been a marked deterioration in Charlie's condition. His breathing became labored; his lungs filled with fluid; his blood oxygen level fell. One of his lungs was partially collapsed, and he had an excess amount of fluid in his lungs and the rest of his body. We had to give him artificial respiration again, as his blood pressure was falling. I think the whole problem is fluid overload. He had not lost enough of the fluid he retained after the surgery on the heart-lung machine. I must give him diuretics to flush out the fluid. If that does not work, he will require re-operation and that would be too risky. I have prayed for him since he was born, and I pray now more than ever: "Lord, he is your child. Let us keep him. Guide us in his therapy. Let us share in your creation. I love him so much. I remember Charlie's smile—a turned up corner of his mouth and a sort of wink with twinkling eyes. Oh, he must stay with us a few more years. He loves life—he has given and received so much love. Think of his mom, dad, grandmoms and granddads. He must live!"

He improves. Today has been free of problems. The blood oxygen is normal. The blood pressure is good. The fluid has not reaccumulated in his lung or tissues. He perseveres in his difficult fight for life. I see the blue eyes awakening from the morphine narcotics. His eyes pierce my heart and soul. They are asking: "What is wrong? Why am I in this place? Why can't you hug me?" I hold his hand and try to tell him, "You are getting better!" He is just a baby, but he clutches my finger in a kind of understanding.

Cathy, his nurse, says, "I can't believe how marvelous he is!" Tomorrow we will try to remove the tube from his trachea and discontinue the respirator.

Day 6: Extubation
Charlie's tube is out. He is breathing without assistance. We returned the respirator to the storeroom. He is pink. He makes sucking and chewing movements with his little mouth as though to remind himself that his lips can come together again. For five days those lips encircled a plastic tube that delivered oxygen to his lungs. I watch his lips, marveling again at the rose color and the rosebud form. His little face is free of the tape which had held the tube in place. I stroke his face, but he cries as I touch him. He is afraid…It will be a few days before he trusts us again and before his enchanting smile returns. I have never seen babies smile until five or six days after surgery, for they are untrusting and fearful; they cannot understand that they are being helped. They can only understand that they are not with mother and father, and that they are not being cuddled. Then "all is forgiven" and that loving sign returns—the smile! It seems sort of miraculous that this recovery takes so little time!

Day 7: Oral Feeding
Charlie is taking his oral feeding. He lurched forth to grab the bottle from the nurse—understandable for one who has not received oral feeding for five days. His mother hovers over him and beams as she holds him—the first time since surgery (seven long days) and her whole being radiates loving maternity, greater perhaps than when she first held him on his day of birth. This is a kind of birth of a new life for a baby who is transformed from sick to well. He relishes her cuddling but does not smile. His confidence is not totally restored and he withholds this ultimate sign of trust and love. I think this will take a few more days, and then his first smile will be for his mother.

Day 8: The Calm After the Storm
His intake is totally by mouth. The intravenous feeding has been discontinued. All his tubes have been removed. He is sleeping peacefully. His respirations are quiet; there is no gasping. He lies quietly with gentle countenance—the calm after the storm.

Day 9: Baby Food
Charlie takes his baby food.

Day 10: Smiling Again
He smiled for his mother! And he does not turn his head from me as before. He stares at me, quizzically, without anger. He is wondering if I am trustworthy...

Day 11: More Comfort
Now I am more comfortable about Charlie. I know he will go home soon. It has been such a long struggle but so worthwhile!

Day 12: Smiling for his Father
Charlie smiled for his father.

Day 16: Accepting Me
Charlie allowed me to hold him and after a short stare of uncertainty he accepted me as his friend and smiled! His mother told me how overwhelmed his father had been on day 12, when he finally received that smile from their son. Father had been so devastated earlier when Charlie turned his head away from him shortly after the surgery—the little fellow's meager but powerful way of punishing his father for his ordeal. Soon Charlie will be discharged.

Day 31: Check-Up Visit After Discharge
Charlie came for his check-up today. It is about one month since his surgery. He glows with health. His blueness is gone. Awareness of health is so heightened when one observes the transformation of a blue child to a rosy one. He smiles with little provocation. Obviously he feels so much better. Everyone comes to see him and rejoices. His mother, ever so sensitive, asks, "Do you

want to hold him?" She invites us to share in the joy of caressing him, of feeling his life-filled little body. Then he smiles again…

CHAPTER 7

Exerting Control By Drawing A Picture Before Surgery

Samantha is a pretty little girl who has an ASD (atrial septal defect), a hole between the upper chambers of the heart. Her mom stayed with her during the pre-operative period. She had many other friends staying with her, including an imaginary dog in her drawer. All of her dolls had hearts with holes in them. I vividly recall asking her if her doll was going to have her hole fixed too. She said, "I'm going to take Dolly to another doctor and the other doctor will give her medicine to fix her heart."

Certainly Samantha was not happy with the sort of doctors who helped sick children in such a frightful operation. It is particularly difficult to convince a child that she needs an operation, when the child feels so well. For most children, an ASD has no symptoms during childhood years. But the surgery is done during childhood to prevent deterioration which may otherwise go unseen until the second or third decade of life. The heart tolerates its extra load for a long time before it begins to fail.

An unusual thing occurred when Samantha arrived in the Operating Room. There was the tiny blue-eyed blonde lying on the operating table. Everyone was tooling up for the procedure. The technicians were setting up the heart-lung machine. The nurses were preparing the instruments. The anesthesiologist was readying all the medication that would be used during the surgery. Just as she was about to place the anesthesia mask on Samantha's face, Samantha said, "Wait a minute, I want to draw a picture!" The anesthesiologist gave her a paper and a marking pen. The child drew an octopus-like figure with holes in it. Then she quietly accepted the mask and went to sleep.

Surely the little one felt like a sacrificial victim, but she had managed to exhibit control over this spectacular event, for she had called a halt to all activity for an important five minutes. That was quite a feat for a four-year-old girl.

CHAPTER 8

A Child's Resentment For His Hospitalization

Jimmy plays and reads and enters into all kinds of mischief. He is fine now; pink, robust and healthy. He has a full life ahead, now that his heart has been repaired.

I remember well the first day I met him. He was four months old, and had done well despite his being born prematurely. He had overcome this handicap, and now he was faced with a second problem. He had been born with a heart defect. I hoped he would be tough enough to conquer this too.

He was admitted to the hospital for a cardiac catheterization, to determine the exact nature of the defect, and to treat his mild heart failure. We found him to have a ventricular septal defect, a hole between the two pumping chambers of the heart. He was treated with Digoxin for the heart failure; he improved and was discharged. But he had an interesting reaction to his hospitalization.

Though Jimmy had been very personable and smiling before admission, he stopped smiling and turned away when his parents visited him. Surely he felt deserted and depressed. After seven days at home, his pre-hospitalization personality returned.

I mention this story so that other parents do not become upset by similar temporary resentments by their hospitalized children. Such reactions are normal and parents should take comfort in knowing that they are passing reactions. Ultimately they will feel contented, knowing they did the right things for their children.

CHAPTER 9

Living With A Pacemaker

Sarah is eleven years old now and was born with a hole between the upper chambers of her heart. The surgeon repaired this defect when Sarah was five years old. After the surgery she developed complete heart block. This means that the electrical impulse of the upper chamber was not being delivered to the lower chamber. Therefore, the heart rate was extremely low and unstable. The surgeon implanted a permanent pacemaker so that her heart could maintain an appropriate heartbeat rate.

Sarah was the sweetheart of the surgical service. The chief resident I'll call Dr. Bob, who on most occasions was rather stern and objective, found it impossible to be objective with Sarah. She became the "blonde of his life." Surgical residents always have an excessive amount of work and very little time to socialize with their patients. But this did not apply to Sarah because she was an irresistibly loving girl who won the hearts of the toughest of surgical teams.

Sarah left the hospital with a battle-scarred chest, one incision for her heart repair and another for the placement of the pacemaker. But nothing stopped this little one, for she was proud of her scars and was free in exhibiting them to her playmates. Having been a fully active child, the pacemaker was not to interfere with her activity. In fact, within a short time after her discharge she was hanging from a tree branch. She continued to be active and at eleven years had won the gymnastics and physical fitness award in her class. This was after another pacemaker had been implanted that year. Fortunately, newer pacemakers are more durable and have a greater longevity.

There are some data that suggest that the child with congenital heart disease suffers from a lack of self-confidence and develops a sense of inferiority, although this did not seem to be the case with Sarah. This sense of inferiority may be imposed on the child by the parents, physicians or teachers, but I believe that if the child is treated like any other child, he/she will have a self-appreciation greater than that of a child with no handicap. Most of the children I have treated have exhibited a gallantry and courage greater than many adults. In spite of their handicaps, these children show us so vividly the value of life as they try to capture every precious moment. Indeed, what is a handicap often becomes a stimulus to find the beautiful things inside each and every one of us.

I have seen inner strength in Sarah and in many other children, some of whom have not lived but have still shown us the beauty and importance of life.

CHAPTER 10

Success After A Stormy Course

Informing Eric's Mother about Cyanotic Congenital Heart Disease
With three kisses on his forehead, I said a happy goodbye. Eric is going home, happy, no longer tired, and pink as a lovely rose. I believe all babies have been kissed by the angels, but Eric must have also had the angels as playmates. The intensity of the remembered moments of his first eight months of life is difficult to totally appreciate.

Eric's life started with many problems. First, he was born as a blue-baby. When he was one day old his doctors had to separate him from his mother to transfer him to a medical center which dealt with heart disease, away from a mother who cherished him.

I remember my call to his mother: "Mrs. Baker, I'm calling from the medical center and I'm sorry that I, a stranger, must tell you so many difficult things. But I must keep you fully informed. Your baby has a serious heart disease and will require a diagnostic procedure called a cardiac catheterization which carries a mortality risk of three to five percent. In other words, your baby has a three to five percent chance of dying during this procedure. He is extremely blue and lacking in oxygen. We must do this procedure to give him a chance at continued life. I must also tell you that it is possible that a surgical procedure carrying a mortality risk of 25 percent may be necessary within the next few days. Again, please forgive me for conveying this information over the telephone."

My own emotions were so mixed, with sympathy for the mother and anxiety and fear for the life and health of the baby. There was hardly a second of pause when the mother answered: "If this is what you have to do to help him, do it. You have my full permission." I valued the trust expressed in these words and I prayed that with God's help we could help this little blue baby.

The catheterization confirmed that the baby had a serious cyanotic congenital heart disease. To improve the baby's oxygen level, we conducted a procedure in the catheterization laboratory to make a hole between the upper two chambers of the heart. This allowed more re-oxygenated blood to reach the rest of his body. The procedure was successful for a short period of time but then the oxygen level fell again. Eric would have to go to surgery. By this time I had met Mrs. Baker and it was a little easier to present this bad news to her since it could be done personally and not by telephone. Again, her response was, "Do whatever you have to do to help my baby." I knew the sadness, fear and worry that underlay this valued expression and I wondered if I could have been so decisive if it had been my own child.

The First Surgery and its Complications
Eric went to surgery and the surgeon created a larger hole between the upper chambers of the heart to allow more oxygenated blood to circulate throughout his body. He hardly had time to enjoy this improvement when he developed a serious infection involving the tissues around the brain and spinal cord: meningitis. Now for the third time Eric's parents heard bad news. And his mother asked me, "Does he have a chance?" After my affirmative response she assured me that he would indeed get well. And he did get well, but a few days after, when the antibiotics were stopped, the meningitis recurred. At this point the risks were tremendous. It was difficult for me to bring such bad news to Eric's parents for a fourth time. How could I say that Eric was likely to die? I did not have to say this to his parents because they understood the situation. They asked me again, "Does he have a chance?" I answered, "Yes, but it is necessary to insert a needle in his brain to see if he has infection there too, and it may be necessary to inject the antibiotics directly into his spinal canal." They gave me permission once again: "Do anything that will help him." After some time Eric recovered. What a magnificent outcome!

He recovered but he later had to face many difficulties. When he was four months of age he developed hydrocephalus (an abnormal amount of fluid in the head, causing swelling), a complication secondary to his early episode of meningitis. Again, he had to be hospitalized and required a shunting procedure so that the obstruction to the flow of spinal fluid could be bypassed. We placed a small tube into the fluid-containing chamber on the inside of his brain, and directed the tube under the skin and into the abdomen to allow drainage of the fluid and relief of his condition. Undoubtedly, this surgery was made more complicated because of Eric's blueness. The heart surgery which had been done earlier was only palliative, that is, a surgery to temporarily improve the situation so that complete repair of the heart could be performed at a later time when Eric would be big enough to tolerate such a comprehensive surgery.

There was a complication after the procedure for hydrocephalus. I think his cyanosis was partly responsible for this complication. Eric had bleeding into his heart. Then he became weak and had difficulty feeding. His little mouth drooped and he could not suck a nipple properly. He was so tired-he had been through so much! We conducted special studies: spinal taps and special brain X-rays among others. Again, he improved and was taken home. He regained his ability to suck. His little mouth regained that survival power and that lovely baby began to suck.

The next two months were quiet, although Eric's blueness was quite significant. He was nearly purple…when he cried his lips were like grapes. He was weak and his motor development was delayed. Yet despite all this, he was very sociable. He smiled with little inducement. He was fascinated by his hands and did not seem to care they were blue. Then when he became seven months old his blueness became even more severe and his fatigue worsened. We had wanted to wait until he was one year old for him to have his big heart surgery, but now it seemed that the surgical date would need to be advanced.

The Second Surgery

Eric was admitted for another cardiac catheterization in preparation for surgery. The clotting factors in his blood were all abnormal. This abnormality was related to his cyanosis but it was worrisome, for it would present a higher risk for catheterization and certainly for surgery. His oxygen level in the blood was only 40 percent. It is phenomenal that he functioned so well considering that the normal blood oxygen level is 95 percent. The catheterization revealed that he had developed a narrowing below the blood vessel which leads to the lungs. This condition added an even higher risk to the heart surgery. Yet, it was a risk that needed to be taken; the baby would not survive very long with such a low oxygen level.

The days preceding the surgery were difficult. We contacted many other cardiac surgeons in an effort to determine if a better approach could be used other than the traditional one. All indicated that the surgery would be very difficult and that there would be a stormy post-operative course. I was pleased when Eric's grandparents came before the surgery, first so they could see their grandson, and secondly so that they could support Eric's mother and father. I had great fears that he would not survive the surgery. I remember kissing him every day and saying a little prayer: "God, take care of him!" Whenever I whispered that prayer he would always smile as though he understood every word.

It was difficult for me to hide my concern on the night before the surgery. I could feel a lump in my throat; I swallowed and hoped that my fears would not be noticed. His grandmother said to me, "He is so beautiful, we can't lose him!" Early the following morning he arrived in the Operating Room with his little binky "pacifier," his two favorite blankets and his love-worn tiger. The anesthesiologist placed a tube in his trachea to control his respiration. His beautiful blue eyes were covered with ointment and his eyelids were closed to protect his eyes during the surgery. His soft strawberry-blond hair was still combed. I touched his head; it felt so cold because his body was being cooled to a low temperature to protect his tissues and to enable the surgery to go easier and faster. Soon he had no heartbeat because the heart-lung machine was working for him.

The surgeon moved very quickly. First, he clipped out the scar tissue that had narrowed the outlet to the lung blood vessel. Then he rearranged the inside of the heart to correct the heart defect. Then he said, "Re-warm him." The blood from the heart-lung machine was warmed and Eric's temperature started to increase. His little heart started to beat, first very slowly and then faster and faster, but still not fast enough. The surgeon said: "Turn on the pacemaker." This was meant to stimulate the heart artificially and to give the heart the necessary number of beats per minute. The pacemaker was turned on...and suddenly Eric's own heartbeat went faster than the pacemaker's. He showed us he did not need the pacemaker! The pacemaker was turned off and Eric's heartbeat continued at an effective rate. "I'm coming off the tube", said the surgeon. Now Eric was halfway on his own power…no trouble. "A total bypass" said the surgeon and now Eric had no help outside his own heart. Five minutes elapsed, then ten minutes, then fifteen and his reconstructed heart was working without any help. His blood was red…it was filled with oxygen! His little face was pink. His hands, his ears were no longer blue. I waited for a full twenty minutes after he was off his heart-lung machine before I called to tell his mother that he was all right. My own heart was full. I was happy and grateful to the Lord who first gave him life, and to the surgeon whom the Lord directed to give Eric life again.

After Eric arrived in the Recovery Room, his mother and father and his grandparents visited. We all rejoiced together, for it was obvious that the surgery had been successful. We celebrated these early moments with caution, for we knew how quickly the situation could change. But all went so well and Eric's breathing tube was removed the very next morning. By that evening he was sucking on a pacifier which had been dipped in honey. He relished it with contentment and security.

Surgical Complications

For the next 12 hours he was doing quite well and showed no signs of breathing difficulty or disturbance of the heart rhythm. But then his blood pressure fell slightly and his heart rate fell slightly. Such occurrences are usually not serious signs, but they were more worrisome when a baby has just had heart surgery. Consequently, many of his physicians gathered around his bedside, observed him closely and discussed the best management for him. We did some of the simple things. We used a pacemaker and were able to make the heart go faster. This helped a little. But within an hour his little lungs filled with water and he began to have extreme difficulty with his breathing. We had to place another tube in his trachea (his own breathing organ) and use a respirator to help eliminate the fluid in the lungs and relieve his effort at breathing. Then we gave him medicine to make him sleep so that he would not resist the respirator.

This situation was a relatively mild setback. Eric's parents understood and seemed prepared for it. Eric always gave us a scare before he got completely better! By next morning, things were much improved. The oxygen in his blood was normal. We tried to "wean" him from the respirator. This means that we allowed him to breathe part of the time and the rest of the time the machine would breathe for him. Eventually, he breathed so well that the tube was removed again. After that, he had no further difficulty and continued to improve and to heal. He went home and smiling two weeks after the surgery.

Success at Last

I saw him ten days later in his little stroller. He was still smiling and happy. His energy was a lot more than it was before. He could cry and not turn purple. He could exercise and not become tired. He could suck on his bottle and not become breathless. Finally, he could really know what it is like to be a healthy baby!

CHAPTER 11

Taking A Chance On A Risky Surgery For A Full Life

A well child is our greatest gratification. Some children are older when their surgery is done. These children are more aware of their limitations and of the magnificent transformation that comes with surgery.

Kevin was nineteen years old when he had heart surgery. When he was an infant, the risk of surgery was high and his parents chose to wait. They waited "until he was of an age to make his own decision". (This situation took place in the early days of heart surgery, and currently such long waits are unwarranted and seldom seen.) Fortunately the waiting did not compromise his chances for a good result from surgery. His early years had been so difficult, for he was blue and could tolerate very little physical activity. He had "spells," his blueness would become more intense, and he would faint. The social embarrassment was almost more difficult for him than the physical discomfort. To avoid embarrassment, he would run and hide when he anticipated a spell.

I loved Kevin as soon as I met him. He was shy, but valiant as he said, "I want to have heart surgery so I can live as I want to live." He was studying graphic design, although his first love was photography. However, the limitations imposed by his heart disease were so severe that he could not pursue his desired field with the vigor it demanded. He had a successful surgery and I had the pleasure of watching his transformation from a blue child to pink.

A few months after surgery, Kevin returned for a re-examination. It was a busy day and I was moving along slowly. I was behind by one to two hours. I was uneasy because I know how difficult it is for children to wait. Yet when I walked into the exam room where Kevin was waiting, his warmth, sensitivity and beautiful revelations drew forth my total concentration. I forgot my hurried state as though he had drawn a circle enclosing us in a protective halo of light.

I enjoyed seeing him and hearing of his "new" life. What a magnificent gift he gave me! He told me of doing those things he could not do as a child. He told me of sledding down a snow-covered hill and skating across the ice without fatigue. He asked about marriage: the question of children and the hereditary nature of his heart defect. He talked with strength and vibrancy, with the awareness of living, really living!

However, he had had a problem in getting a job. Who would have anticipated a problem now that there were basically no limitations on his activity? Yet the reality was there. He was told by a prospective employer, "You may look healthy but you have a scar on your chest; you have had heart surgery; we may be taking a chance." The letter that I had dictated to this employer had said: "Kevin has had an excellent repair of his heart defect. He may be allowed full activities with the exception of competitive sports." Those last six words, "with the exception of competitive sports," alarmed the employer, and it was several months before he granted the position to Kevin. This made me think about the significance of a job: how little a job is appreciated by many, yet how much it is valued by those with medical restrictions!

How wonderful it was to read his letter written three years after his surgery. It said: "I thought you might like the enclosed original. This was my first photo to be published." The photo was entirely appropriate. It depicted a sleeping tiger kitten lying inside a basket. On the outside of the basket there was an adult tiger, and the caption stated: "When you dream, dream big!" Kevin's big dreams were being realized. He mentioned in his letter that his bicycle had traveled 3000 miles in one year. This was a feat of great magnitude for anyone.

I wonder if Kevin realized that the gift of his triumph was also my own. I could not imagine a greater one. His existence makes me happy, and the individual details of his actions make me even happier. Many years later I could picture him skating, skiing, biking...participating in all of nature!

PART III
SADNESSES AND EMERGING HOPES

CHAPTER 12

"Rainy Days Make Flowers Grow"

Julie was in the Intensive Care Unit and there was little that could be done for her. She had lost an immense amount of weight. She was very thin and yet her eyes were beautiful. Her little comments made us ashamed that we had not enjoyed and appreciated life more. I said to her: "Julie, perhaps tomorrow you can go to the outdoors playroom, won't that be nice? I'm sure it will be a beautiful sunny day for you." Then I thought, "How could I even think that a little child would appreciate a beautiful sunny day when she is dying?" Yet, here was her answer: "But the rainy days are nice too! The rain makes the flowers grow!" I was so taken by the perceptive power of this suffering angel child. In her handicap she taught me the preciousness of life, which sadly she soon lost.

CHAPTER 13

Clinging To Life As A Sibling Is Born

Betty has been dying for a month now but fights to stay alive. She forces her eyes open and sits up most of the time. She is still interested in her games. Her brother Mike received a new one last Thursday for his birthday. Betty had to try it. Though her little head nods from fatigue, she still musters up enough enthusiasm to enjoy the two clown dolls her grandmother has brought her. Both dolls are smiling. But Betty's face is sad and wasted. Her eyes are circled and her face shows its bony structure. She is thin but her legs are inflated with fluid from heart failure. Now she has fluid in her chest and her breathing is labored. It must be close. Death must be coming soon.

Today is Saturday. Betty slept better since receiving the Demerol. June is taking care of her today. This temporary improvement has happened often, but today it is important because Betty's mother has gone to another hospital to give birth. Her contractions are ten minutes apart. Betty's father is with Betty's mother.

Dear Lord, thank you for extending Betty's life until her family is blessed with another new life, and her father can be back at Betty's bedside!

CHAPTER 14

Condolence Letter: "The Gift Of Love Never Dies"

Dear Mr. and Mrs. Jones,

I have thought of you often since little Andy's death. The loss is so great, as though a part of your being were missing.

There are many questions: Why sickness? Why death? And why both in a beautiful newborn baby? The answers are not there. But one thing is certain: there is an infinite gift which Andy brought that cannot die. It is the gift of love and, yes, it is the gift of life.

First, he is the fruit of your love. I say "is" because that love still exists. It continues in itself and in the love you have for each other and for your family. It is the gift of life because he has taught us more about its value than many others who have lived for eighty years.

In his short months he has helped us appreciate the value of every touch, of every smile, of all that is seen, heard and tasted. We no longer take any of this for granted, for we are now so aware of how these "ordinary things" of life are very special.

We must continue an appreciation, which he taught us, by committing to even fuller loves and fuller lives for ourselves and those who are close to us.

And so, in his death he lives in our capacity to love and in the lives we value.

I am never as aware of life as when I have seen death. Realize how much I share your loss. I hope my thoughts will help you at this most difficult time.

CHAPTER 15

Condolence Letter: "Our Comitment To Living Should Be Greater For Having Loved Him"

Dear Mr. and Mrs. Smith,

I appreciate your letter and I send you my deepest sympathy. I cried for your loss and for our loss. It is strange how close I felt to Bobby despite our rather brief encounter.

His yearly Christmas messages were brief but said much more than he wrote. He spoke of love, hope, commitment and an appreciation of life which is known to too few.

I weep as I write this letter, for he who possessed such understanding is gone, but this is his legacy to those who knew him. Our love, our hope and our commitment to living are greater for having known him.

I thank God for Bobby and I thank Bobby for the gifts of himself that he has left us.

PART IV
THE CHILD AS SEEN BY HIM/HERSELF, PARENTS AND DOCTOR

CHAPTER 16

Dealing With Anxiety

GRACE TELLS GEORGE'S STORY

After George was admitted to the hospital, I conducted a physical examination and noticed a heart murmur. I then made a diagnosis of atrial septal defect. It is not unusual for this defect to escape detection until a child is in the pre-adolescent years. I arranged for a cardiac catheterization to confirm my clinical diagnosis. The catheterization revealed that the defect was of a size which would require surgery.

George was anxious about the surgery. He chatted incessantly and was very fidgety. I recall especially a situation two nights before the scheduled surgery. George's mother was standing at the elevator crying and she said, "I didn't let him see me cry; he is so upset already!" I promised I would look in on him before I went home.

I walked into George's room and found him a little tearful, but mostly angry. He was talking about war (he was something of a war buff and knew a great deal about World War II). He said to me, "If I could just get out of here for a short while I would get a hand grenade and blow up this place." He also said, "I could go to the arsenal downtown and start a war." I asked him, "George, on which side would I be, with you or against you?" He paused and then said (as if not to hurt my feelings), "On my side." I then asked him who he would fight in the war. He said, "I would fight a girl in my class because nobody likes her anyway." Then he started telling me about flying coffins. I was puzzled, and later a colleague enlightened me that some airplanes in World War II were called flying coffins.

I believe that George, in his war stories, conveyed his feelings of anger, anxiety and fear. Certainly most children have similar feelings but are not able to convey them in the vivid manner George portrayed. There were only two days left before the surgery and it seemed not enough time to allay the anxieties of this lovely boy. I sought the assistance of one of our pediatric psychiatrists to help me handle the situation.

George's conversation with the psychiatrist revealed information which was important to convey to my colleagues and myself: feelings to which we had not sufficiently tuned in. George drew a picture of his conception of the heart and heart surgery. It showed George's image of the "defective heart". Obviously he was aware that the "hole" in his heart was in the upper chambers. A square-like projection around the heart represented George's concept of the heart-lung machine, or in his words, the "hook-up". He had seen a movie in which hook-ups had been displayed. After drawing the picture George stated that what worried him the most was the tube in his mouth, which would be placed during the course of the surgery and remain in place for about 12 hours thereafter. He was fearful because he would not be able to talk.

Another drawing showed a "raindrop." To us, this drawing told the whole story, as it seemed to us that the drop was like a large "tear". This symbol seemed to embody all those emotions which we have associated with tears: sadness, fear, anger, loneliness. The loneliness theme appeared prominently in his expressions. Earlier he had referred to the "flying coffins" of World War II which probably suggested fear that he would not come out of the surgery alive. Some of his other "loneliness" symbols included a "missile base" (for space travel), which was the same shape as the drawing of his heart. I found some encouragement in this drawing, since most of the space adventures in our country had been successful ones, thus suggesting that perhaps this symbol might be showing some optimism.

Most medical personnel who deal with children are quite aware of the anxiety a child suffers when he approaches surgery, or even on any occasion when he leaves the security of home for a hospital setting. However, I believe the anxiety, fear and loneliness associated with heart surgery is probably one of the most powerful, for most children who have reached the age of reason are quite aware of the importance of the heart. And the entertainment media have augmented this childhood awareness via the many programs, both educational and "entertaining" which involve the study of the heart and heart surgery.

This is why it was so important that George to talk to the surgeon, who fortunately made a hugely favorable impression on him. I had informed the surgeon that George was most anxious and fearful and asked him to try to allay George's anxieties. Somehow, I feel that the tall stature and self-confidence of the surgeon alone conveyed confidence to George. Also, the surgeon took extra time to explain to his patient that he had nothing to fear. He told George that during World War II he had been an evacuation medical officer in the Normandy landing beaches, and that he had saved the lives of all his patients. Imagine how meaningful this story was to a child already spellbound by war stories! Furthermore, it so happened that the surgeon's middle name was also George, and this coincidence established an additional bond.

In short, George's encounter with the surgeon was powerful and positive. In this case, George had the good fortune to have a surgeon willing enough to take time to talk. Perhaps this surgeon was particularly sensitive to the needs of children, as he was the father of a large family. I believe little children need to see and interact with the "big man" or "big woman" who is directly responsible for their lives. If that person exudes confidence this makes the child at ease. Every surgeon should try to put their little patients at ease!

I have found myself detailing the story of George in particular because it most vividly exemplifies the entire emotional framework of a child about to undergo surgery. The story related by his mother, below, will show you another perspective and tells you of the fortunate results…

GEORGE'S MOTHER TELLS HER SON'S STORY

God gave us our son twice: first on the day he was born and then a decade later, on the day he had successful heart surgery to repair a hole in his heart.

When George was a year old, our beloved family doctor told us he had detected what was probably an innocent heart murmur. I can remember him saying, "I'm telling you this so that when he goes to school and the school nurse calls you and tells you about the murmur she found, you can tell her that I was already aware of it." The doctor was right in one respect: when George was in first grade the school nurse called me and questioned the murmur. I told her the doctor believed it was harmless. That seemed to be the end of it. It wasn't until almost a decade later that we discovered otherwise.

The troubles started when George was bothered with diarrhea for several weeks. When numerous visits to a local doctor did nothing to stop it, the doctor recommended a specialist at a major medical center. He examined George and suggested that he be hospitalized for tests. I was puzzled by how many of the doctors seemed to be listening to his heart. I can remember thinking, "They all are looking at the wrong place…he has diarrhea!" This is when Dr. Grace Wolff examined him. Then she called me out in the hall and in a very gentle manner explained that George had a hole in his heart and that it needed to be treated. She indicated that it was not an urgent matter and that we could wait until his other problems were cleared up. She spoke to me so calmly that I found myself feeling that she surely didn't mean "open heart surgery"! Those three words seemed so ominous! But my worst fears were confirmed when the first specialist spoke with me later, asking if Dr. Wolff had told me of the heart condition, adding gently: "You know, it's about this open heart surgery you hear about."

I remember breaking the news to John, George's father. Neither of us was expecting to hear anything like that! Afterwards Dr. Wolff spoke to George, as did we. It was necessary to tell him. So miraculous was Dr. Wolff's manner with children that George was not alarmed, at least not initially. That night we told other members of our family.

George spent nearly two weeks in the hospital at that time, a difficult experience for a child who had never been away from home. The condition for which he was hospitalized was diagnosed as proctitis (a digestive system condition), which required follow-up treatment for another three years. We were grateful that this condition required his hospitalization; otherwise his heart condition might have gone undetected for a long time.

George's proctitis was controlled adequately by medication and it became time for us to take him to the hospital for a cardiac catheterization to confirm if surgery was necessary. My husband John underwent surgery around that time. It was on the day of his surgery that I received a notice from the hospital that George's appointment was in a few days. Because John required some days of recovery time at the hospital, we decided to postpone the catheterization for a few more days. The anticipation of this procedure was difficult for all of us. For George the worst part of his trips to the hospital was not the treatments; he complained mostly about being away from home. He was a real homebody. And for us, leaving him alone at nights was one of the hardest aspects of his hospitalization.

We were told not to come until about noon on the day of the catheterization. When we arrived he was sleeping in his room. John stayed a little while but then had to leave to go back to work. After the procedure, a young doctor came in and told me that Dr. Wolff would be in shortly to tell me "What, if anything, had to be done." I said, "It's the 'if anything' that I'm hoping for." He quickly responded, "Oh, I don't know, not the way the blood is going through there." I felt I had my answer. Indeed when Dr. Wolff came, she explained that surgery would be required. She reassured me that the surgical success rate was high and said we would hear from the surgeon to arrange for an appointment to see him. I remember our Minister had stopped in before Dr. Wolff came. He had prayed with me and I remember shedding tears.

A few days later we took George to the hospital for an examination and to find out when the operation would be. We had a 45-minute wait in a tiny room where they set broken bones. There was no window and the plaster-splattered walls were all lined with crutches, saws for cutting casts, etc. George was scared and said simply, "Let's go home!" We felt the same way…except that we knew we could not go! Finally a doctor examined him and then sent us to a pleasant young woman who arranged his surgical date. He was to be admitted to the hospital three days before the surgery. She told us he would be in the Intensive Care Unit at first, with a total of about two weeks of hospitalization. The words "intensive care" frightened George; he did not know what they meant. I know he was so worried about it all. He said, "This is the last time. I'll take pills and go to the doctor, but I won't go back to the hospital after this." We so hoped he would be right.

I can probably best relate our feelings the next month by copying the words from my diary three days before his admission:

Dear Diary,

Flag Day, and the last day of school for George. It doesn't seem possible he'll be going in three days from now, after a year of thinking about it. The darned clock just keeps ticking, and all things come eventually. It seems to be saying, "Ready or not…" I wonder if we ever would truly be ready. George breaks my heart. He tries so hard to cope, yet nights after he goes to bed seem to be worse…he talks about different aspects of the surgery and you just know he's wondering and frightened. He seems more concerned about the hospital stay than about the operation. I tell my sister Peggy that I don't know what to say to George any more. She replies that I can't lie to him and tell him it will be fun. Sometimes George calls me in the night and hangs on to me so! Not for a minute am I ungrateful that this surgery can be done, but I can't say I'm happy. Thank goodness I know God will take care of him. So many people have assured us of their prayers, and that means a lot! These past two weeks have been very hard for him. Now today when I realize this is his last day of school and he gets admitted to the hospital in three days, all I want to do is eat and cry, neither of which will help, neither of which I need. How fortunate we'll feel when I can write and say it's over!

The day before we went to the hospital we took George to see his grandmother at the nursing home. From the wheelchair she hugged him and fought back tears! I have come to admit that some things in life are too hard. Our hearts ached for him too! The morning we were to leave for the hospital he hugged his two cats so tightly before he left!

When we arrived at the hospital a nurse called for a lunch tray for George. He did not eat; she was not pleased. She snapped, "Well, you're not going to be very popular around here!" A bad start for a sensitive child who was so scared to begin with! I hasten to add that this brief incident was the only exception to otherwise very caring attitudes by all other nurses and doctors.

George cried so much at nights after we left. I was so sorry that he had to be up there three days before the surgery; I feel he really got more upset during that time. One of the nurses explained that part of the reason for the long pre-operative stay was to get George accustomed to the hospital. Still, I felt that considering that this was his third trip within a year, and that for him the hardest part was being away from home, the three-day stay had made things more difficult. When I told Dr. Wolff about George's fright, she was most helpful. She immediately told the surgeon. The surgeon was wonderful. He spoke so nicely to George the day before the surgery, and also had us meet two little girls and their parents. He had operated on the girls, and it was so reassuring to see their progress. It all helped a lot...

John and I were awake by 4:00 A.M. on the day of the operation, and we were at the hospital by 8:00 A.M. Dr. Wolff called us halfway through the surgery to say that George had gone on the heart-lung machine and that the surgeon was about to sew up the hole. Shortly after 12:00 noon Dr. Wolff came out to tell us the operation had gone well. She told us the hole had been about the size of a quarter, and that the surgeon had closed it. She also told us what to expect to see when we went to see George in the ICU. The surgeon called on the "hot line" and told us to wait about 45 minutes before going to the ICU. Our Minister had joined us; we went to get a sandwich at the cafeteria. John and I made a few calls to reassure some of our relatives. I also called the nursing home and asked to speak directly with my mother to tell her the surgery was successfully over.

But all the while I had one feeling in my mind: I simply wanted to see George, just to look at him myself! The 45-minute wait seemed unending! I now reflect on the preparation I was given for what to expect to see. I guess no one can ever really prepare an inexperienced person for the person's first visit to a post-operative patient at an ICU. The doctor's efforts to calm me had so reassured me that I did not expect the sight to be as involved as it was... so many tubes, wires, etc. As I think back now, I am grateful to my nephew. At the time he was a teenager and shortly before George's surgery he told me bluntly, with the candid honesty of a young person, "He's going to have a scar from here to here!", running his hand up and down his chest. I remember thinking that it could not be, that he must be exaggerating! However, when I first saw George at the ICU with a large bandage going up and down his chest I thought about my nephew's statement and was glad he had made it.

George was crying when we came into the ICU. I swallowed hard, took a tissue and reached under the oxygen mask to wipe his tears. He said softly, "It hurts." My heart ached so hard for him, it also hurt. I am ashamed to admit that when I first saw him lying there I felt for an instant, "We should have let him have his expected thirty years of life and not do this." Now I know how wrong I was. We cannot play God and we should be grateful that the medical profession can do so much. I talked to George quietly until they asked us to leave. When I got outside I leaned against a wall and really cried. John said, "Why are you crying so much?" I said simply, "Because he hurts."

(I recall that the next day a mother came in to see her child and fainted. Another mother told me she couldn't even get herself to go in the ICU for three days to see her daughter. I guess I didn't do too badly!)

We sat in the waiting room. Despite all the reassurances I felt so completely miserable. My little boy "hurt" and it all seemed too much. Dr. Wolff came later and suggested we leave to get rest at home, saying she would call us there later. We left the hospital at about 7:00 P.M., and Dr. Wolff called us with an update at the end of her workday… at 10:00 P.M.! Small wonder we will always love her.

George was in the ICU for five days. The care was marvelous, and the staff was so wonderful to him and to us. They would even come to the waiting room and get us before the regularly scheduled time, and often let us stay with him far longer than we dared to hope. It seemed that each day we went in, a different tube had been removed. They had him sitting up in a chair the day after surgery, and walking before it seemed possible to us. The nurse would walk along the corridor with him, wheeling the device which held the different tubes and wires. George did not like walking in that hall with so many sick people in sight. As a dear little Chinese nurse said to me, "George does not like this…we only see the sickest people in these rooms."

The waiting room was something else again. We heard so many sad stories! Because we aren't people who dwell on illness in every detail, at times it was very difficult to hear relatives recalling every little aspect of each patient's recovery. But hearing these stories made us more grateful for our own successful tale; and we found ourselves worrying and wondering about the other patients. I have always felt that God places people and events in our paths for a reason. I could write volumes about the other patients and their families, and how they touched our lives and we touched theirs.

George had dreaded being in the ICU, but when it was time to go to a regular room he did not want to leave; everyone had been so kind to him where he was. That next week was a long though uneventful one for George, who wanted only to go home. He continued to do so well. We couldn't believe how fortunate we were. I remember meeting a lady in the hall who had visited with me in the waiting room upstairs; her father was dying and she was so sad! I felt selfish for being happy about George's progress.

When we came in at the end of the second week of his stay, I could see that George was unhappy. Somehow he felt he would be discharged that day, but since the stitches had not been removed he was not allowed to leave. That was a long and difficult day. As I said when the six-year old roommate was crying to go home one day, "There is no sick like homesick!"

But the next day George was all smiles. The stitches had been removed, the doctor had put a few of them in a paper cup as souvenirs, and he was coming home! I don't remember ever being happier than that day. We waited to see Dr. Wolff to find out what George would be allowed to do when he got home. She explained everything so nicely…and we were on our way.

As we left the hospital, emotions ran so deep they were hard to express. We had such a feeling of gratitude about what had been successfully accomplished. We had a special feeling of concern for those we were leaving, knowing how we would wonder how their cases had turned out. Still, could not contain our happiness. I do believe we were the happiest people on earth at that moment.

George is fine now. We are all aware of the miracle of his life. I have heard the expression, "You can't appreciate the heights until you have explored the depths." I felt that in a short period of two weeks we had done both. Now we were so grateful to all who made the "heights" possible.

CHAPTER 17

Value Of Maternal Observations And Judgments

GRACE TELLS RICHARD'S STORY

I first saw Richard when he was about five months old. There were no apparent difficulties but his pediatrician, at times, thought that he looked mildly blue, that is, cyanotic (blood which is low in oxygen). When I saw Richard I was not certain about the cyanosis but, because of abnormal findings in the electrocardiogram, we scheduled him for a cardiac catheterization.

The study revealed a severe heart defect in which all four chambers of the heart are normally developed and the main blood vessel to the body, the aorta, is normally developed but the first part of the main blood vessel to the lung is not properly developed. Also, there was a large hole between the lower chambers of the heart. Consequently, the remainder of the blood vessels to the lungs were very small and received their blood supply from other sources, namely collateral blood vessels which had enlarged in an effort to make up for insufficient blood supply to the lungs. Unfortunately, in time these blood vessels had become insufficient to supply Richard with enough blood to his lungs and he became progressively more cyanotic. Accordingly, it became necessary to perform an operation to improve the blood flow to the lungs.

Generally, this operation is not considered very risky, but in Richard's case the blood vessel to the lung was so small that the chances for success were significantly lessened. The surgery went well, but Richard showed little improvement in his few post-operative days. All the physicians caring for him were doubtful that the operation had been successful. Interestingly, though, his mother insisted that he looked so much better. In light of these doubts, we performed another cardiac catheterization in which we injected a tracer substance into the surgically created conduit, and took X-rays. The X-rays proved that there was good blood flow into the lung blood vessels via the new conduit. So the mother was right! This incident and other such incidences continued to reinforce my respect for a mother's assessment of her own child. So often we are inclined to disregard maternal observations and judgments.

I recall the day of the catheterization very well. I was so triumphant to see that the surgery had been successful that I invited the mother to review the X-rays together with me! The successful operation was important for two reasons. First, it would allow Richard to live a more normal life, to have more energy, and to be able to play as a normal little boy. Second, it would provide a possibility for Richard to have a complete correction of his heart defect in the future, which would extend his life expectancy for many years.

As I think of Richard and his parents I concentrate on his parents. I realize how optimistic they appeared and yet I knew how aware they were of the reality of the situation and the possibility of ultimate failure. Richard improved so much after the surgery. He was able to climb and play and run, and to enjoy doing things that little boys love. And yet, there was apprehension because, surely, he would again become fatigued and more cyanotic. We were hoping that over time his lung blood vessels would grow sufficiently so that he might have another operation to correct his heart.

That time is approaching as he enters his sixth year of age. His mom writes: "I am anxiously awaiting the time. He is beginning to compare himself with other kids, and says, 'Why can't I race like Paul? He's my age!' Richard is so neat! He's thoroughly ready to get his ticker fixed so he can keep up with everyone else!"

Before discussing Richard's ultimately favorable outcome at the end of this chapter, I first share writings from Richard's mother...

RICHARD'S MOTHER TELLS HER SON'S STORY
The long-awaited birth of my beautiful baby boy seems clouded by events of fear, anxiety and apprehension that something might be wrong. Looking back on that time, I feel I lived in such naivete and trust in the Lord and others that

I denied any likelihood of imperfection.

What seemed to be an ideal pregnancy with little morning sickness and no signs of trouble, ended in a very frightening state. Richard did not seem to want to be born. Eventually, after being two weeks overdue, an induced labor and a very easy delivery, my 6-pound son arrived. But he seemed exceptionally tired. Each time he was brought to me, he slept rather than ate. After three days of declining my breast and anything the nurses offered him, I was alarmed by the pediatrician. He informed me, "You have a very tired baby here and he's not going home till he eats." I thought he could have been more tactful. Here was the first of many decisions I would make in the next 2 years. Immediate fear and concern for the welfare of my son took over. I decided to go home to tend to the needs of my 6-year old daughter, and leave the care of this sleepy baby to professionals.

At the hospital the baby was fed via bottle so that his intake could be monitored, and I resorted to a breast pump so I would be able to nurse him when he came home. This plan appeared to work well, for three days later Richard came home to join our family. The very first feeding was a delight for both of us, since he nursed hungrily and steadily, and slept peacefully afterward. My fears subsided and I set about the task of caring for my newborn son.

As I mentioned earlier, I lived through a period of naivete, or maybe it was just denial. In retrospect, there were signs through the first few weeks which I shrugged off. The baby slept a lot! He seemed to just nurse and sleep, with very few periods of alertness. His feet were always cold and at times they were so blue that they seemed almost black. One day when Richard's feet were sticking out of the blanket, I recall my husband saying, "Gee, his feet are awfully blue!" I innocently asked, "What could cause that?" He replied, "A circulation problem." "Oh, he's probably just cold", I remarked, and once again discounted the information that had been accumulating. It wasn't long, though, before reality hit hard and had to be dealt with.

I had been taking Richard to the pediatrician's office for checkups every couple of weeks. On one of these visits, I recall the doctor raised a suspicion of a chest cold and sent me to the hospital with Richard for X-rays and blood work. He told me the reason was just to be sure no germs were present in the lungs. Three days later the truth of the matter surfaced. The pediatrician had not been suspicious of a chest cold but of a heart defect. Richard's heart was enlarged. Immediately we made an appointment at the Pediatric Cardiology Clinic at the hospital.

The next few months were a nightmare. I recall a period of almost incapacitation. I cried very often, prayed diligently, wished for miracles. None of these activities eased my distress. Friends and family were very comforting, but all of us were scared. The baby had seemed so perfect...why would something go wrong? I had been so happy to have a son. How could this happen to me? How could God be so cruel? I questioned my values and trusts. I tried to attend to other obligations, but the emotional stress was horrific! What added to the nightmare was that no one knew exactly what was wrong. The X-rays and cardiographs showed imperfection, but just what was causing it, the doctors didn't know. To complicate the diagnosis, Richard didn't even have a heart murmur, which almost all babies with heart defects have.

The doctors finally decided to perform a cardiac catheterization to pinpoint the defect. Following that procedure, Richard was diagnosed as having pulmonary artresia. His pulmonary arteries leading from the heart to the lungs had never completely formed, thereby causing an insufficient supply of oxygen in his blood. Hence, his blueness. Fortunately, as compensation, nature had supplied him with scores of additional small arteries which momentarily seemed to be alleviating the problem. He also had a hole between the lower chambers of the heart which miraculously was working to his advantage. So the questions seemed to be answered. Now we were faced with need to get the problem solved. I think it was then, with the confirmation of the damage and the exactness of the diagnosis, that I was finally able to pull myself together and face the problem head on!

We decided to wait things out awhile, since Richard was not in immediate danger. The doctors wanted to give him some time to grow and become stronger before attempting surgical repair. Meantime, should Richard show signs of stress, a conduit ("shunt") could be implanted which would give him the additional oxygen he might need.

The next year went by with very little trauma. I was able to accept the situation. I made the decision that this beautiful little boy would enjoy life for however long the Lord saw fit for him to live and that I, in turn, would enjoy him for however long I had him. I treated him with plenty of love and tender loving care, and allowed him to do whatever he wanted. I was advised against setting limits of activity, as he was already setting his own. I carefully observed his behavior and was pleased with all he was able to do.

It wasn't until Richard was 18 months that he appeared to be in real trouble. It was then that he couldn't walk very far without stopping to rest. He breathed heavily and would often ask to be picked up. He also appeared more blue than usual. At that age, he was still taking three naps a day. I felt I needed to take some steps. I called the doctor, shared my suspicions about severe difficulties, and set up an immediate appointment. Following that visit, Richard underwent another cardiac catheterization. The results were frightening. He was functioning at a 60-70 percent oxygen level, surprisingly low for what he was able to do. The tiny conduits that were supposed to be his pulmonary arteries hadn't become any larger since the catheterization performed over a year before. Unless these conduits could be widened in some way, total surgical repair was out of the question. The doctors gave me what seemed to be a bleak picture. They informed me that Richard had only a fair chance of surviving the surgery, but that if I did not choose to have the surgery performed, Richard would probably not live beyond his early teens and would in the meantime be very limited in his activity. To me, there seemed to be no choice but to take a chance. I also felt deeply that this child had surmounted many obstacles already and seemed to have a strong will to survive.

I think the day of his surgery was the longest day of my life. Richard was wheeled off in the early morning sleeping soundly as a kitten. The next time I saw him was eight hours later. The doctor kept me very well informed till about 1:00 P.M., after that there was no more news from the operating room. The last two hours of waiting seemed the longest. Finally the ordeal was over and I was taken to the Intensive Care Unit to see my son. Surrounded by tubes, tapes, bottles, machines, etc., was this beautiful breathing baby boy who was very much alive. He could scarcely open his eyes but whimpered with recognition when he saw me. His first response seemed to be joy, but then a scowl appeared on his face. He withdrew from my touch as if to say, "How could you do this to me?"

I understood his mixed emotions, for I too felt pain and anger for his having to go through this suffering, as well as happiness that he had survived the trauma of surgery. I could hardly tear myself away from his bedside when the nurses requested that we leave. But I knew we had made the right decision, for the worst was over now. It was not totally over, though, because the following few days were marred by the questions, "Was the shunt working? Had all this pain been in vain?"

Richard very quickly made an initial recovery from surgery and was out of the ICU in three days. I immediately packed my bags and we began our stay on the floor together. I noticed a definite improvement in Richard's color and behavior. He seemed less blue…his toenails were actually pink! He could also walk to the end of the hall without showing signs of stress. I was delighted and excited about the results. Unfortunately, the doctors were not so pleased, based on their scientific observations.

The doctors questioned my stated improvement in Richard's color and were unable to hear a heart murmur, which would have confirmed the success of the surgery to them. It was their contention that if the shunt were working, the sound of the blood rushing through it should be audible.

Once again, fear set in. Dear God, would this ordeal ever end? I argued with myself, though. I knew there was a favorable change in Richard. I knew my child well enough. But I agreed to have an angiogram performed to settle the matter. To my delight, the doctors were back within an hour and confirmed my belief that Richard was better. They found that the shunt was working and the oxygen level had increased by 10 percent in one week. We got ready to go home.

That was about two years ago. Richard has continued to grow and lead a fairly normal life. He attends a nursery school/day care center, plays with other children, runs and rides his bike. He even skates for short periods of time. No one would ever know the seriousness of his condition by looking at him. He appears as any healthy youngster. However, it seems he gets more than his share of colds and he does tire more easily than other children. There are still times when Richard appears blue, but this happens when he is under a lot of physical stress such as fatigue, over-activity or when he is ill.

Richard's development seems to have progressed at a normal rate, with the exception of language. He did not talk much until he was nearly four years old. I enrolled him in the nursery/day care center with the high hopes that contact with other children would encourage him to talk. It worked! Within a few months Richard was talking normally. Being around that many children presented a higher risk for catching a cold. But on balance it was a positive experience, despite frequent colds. I did not want Richard to be raised differently than other children.

On my daughter Sylvia's part, it was difficult enough for her at her to adapt to a new baby at home after she had been the center of attention for so long. Richard's illness, too, made matters worse, drawing more attention away from her and towards him. Richard and I had to spend a great amount of time and energy in doctors' offices and hospitals. I kept Sylvia informed, always answered her questions, and gave her permission to express her feelings. I always encouraged verbal expression, particularly verbal expressions of emotions, for I believe that only when they are verbalized can they be dealt with. There are times when she is very angry and screams, "Why does he always have to be sick?", especially when sickness interferes with her schedule. But more often, she has learned to accept the situation, own her internal feelings and bring them out into the open. I believe that even adults have similar feelings of anger which must be aired before they can attempt to accept and handle the reality of a situation.

My relationship with my husband did not take the same reasonable course, unfortunately. The tension and strain of Richard's illness accentuated our own communication problems. My husband seemed to have great difficulties handling Richard's problems. Even when he was present physically, I felt an element of separateness. My husband and I are no longer together. I thought that something as emotionally draining as watching our child risk his life would have brought us together, but instead it pushed us apart.

Richard will soon be entering the hospital again for a catheterization to re-evaluate the shunt. If the vessels are large enough, surgery will be scheduled for total repair. I have some fright, but no more than anyone feels when surgery is in order. I am anxious to have this ordeal finished, and a total correction would give me that. As for Richard, he is prepared. He is well acquainted with his doctors and the hospital, and is well aware of what has to be done. We play hospital and doctor and pretend to fix his "ticker". We are both anxious for the time when he will be able to ride a two-wheeler alone and not get tired when he hikes or plays games.

This has been a painful but growing experience for me. With Richard coming so close to death, I have come to value my own life as well as those of my children. I have arranged my own priorities and put my life in order. The doctors who cared for my child have renewed my faith in mankind. They really care and do give their utmost. I value my friends and family who have supported me, and I know I could never have done it without them. The job is not finished yet, but I feel secure in my own capabilities, trust the judgment of the physicians, and leave the rest to the Lord, who has seen fit to give Richard's life, so far.

GRACE DISCUSSES GOOD FINAL OUTCOME

Shortly after I received Richard's mother's story, Richard had complete surgical repair. I spoke with him after his surgery. He triumphantly told me, "My toes and fingers are pink and I already rode a bicycle at the hospital!" This remark came just one week after surgery. Even greater joy lies in store for this little dynamo!

Several months before the operation, Richard sent me a picture he had drawn in school, a green "ink blot", a kind of Rorschach psychological symbol. He titled it "A Baby Butterfly"-so hopeful a sign despite his acknowledged fear. I recall trying to maintain a similar faith in his successful outcome. And yet I was afraid that his lung blood vessels would be too small for a complete repair. I had to force my concentration on his hopeful baby green butterfly. I tried to believe that this rapture with living would defy death.

The symbolic optimism of that baby butterfly is now a reality. Richard enters a new world with the same abandon that characterizes the butterfly-he samples the world with old assurance and newfound ease.

CHAPTER 18

Foster Parents Become Adoptive Parents Upon A Child's Heart Illness

GRACE TELLS RACHEL'S AND HER PARENTS' STORY

I remember the first time I met Rachel. She was four months old. She had been living with her foster mother and father, Judy and Fred. The county's Welfare Department was conducting placement and permanent adoption proceedings. Rachel was found to have heart disease and was admitted for cardiac catheterization when she was five months of age. What a beautiful child! She looked like a little princess with huge brown eyes and her lovely, ivory-white skin.

The cardiac catheterization revealed that she had a most unusual heart defect. The pulmonary veins (the blood vessels which bring oxygen-rich blood to the heart) were draining into the wrong side of the heart. The medical term for this defect is total anomolysis pulmonary venus drainage. After the catheterization, Rachel was put on Digoxin, a medication to improve the func-tion of her heart. She was discharged to the care of her foster parents, with surgery anticipated for the near future.

Rachel's foster parents were very interested in permanent adoption. How-ever, the adoption agency was concerned because of her cardiac problem. Cer-tainly there were no contraindications to adopting a child with heart disease, but the concern was whether the future parents would be sufficiently prepared for the risky surgery, which was anticipated in a few months. (This story took place over thirty years ago, when common practice was delaying surgery until a child's size would better fit the size of the then-available heart-lung machines; today this size matching is no longer an issue.)

Rachel's next few months were difficult. She began to have persistent coughing at night and during nap time. I see my notes which state: "She was a happy, beautiful baby in her usual good humor." My notes further indicate that we were making every effort to "nurse" this baby along until she reached an older age in which surgical risk would be reduced. I suggested that the infant be placed in an upright position in a little infant seat during her naptime and night-time sleep. Also, I instituted two other medications to assist in the relief of her persistent congestive heart failure.

Afterwards, Rachel's next few months were fairly good, except for the persistence of her rapid breathing and of her vomiting. Her very conscientious foster mother altered her diet so that she was fed infant food, and thereby she had less of a problem with vomiting. On her next visit, Rachel exhibited signs of easy fatiguing with feeding, and some mild blueness. She developed a respiratory infection two months later, and following that she had a significant worsening of her congestive heart failure. Her chest X-ray showed increasing enlargement of the heart and accordingly she was admitted to the hospital for surgery when she became a year old.

Rachel was wheeled into the Operating Room on Valentine's Day. All of us in the medical team were very tense and very concerned, but the surgery went beautifully. I vividly recall all the anxieties preceding the surgery, and as I recall the day of surgery I see that beautiful little body "lost in a large bed" in the Pediatric Intensive Care Unit, her arms and legs restrained and her respirations controlled with a special ventilator. I could see that when her foster parents came into the room, they were devastated by seeing all the equipment surrounding their little girl. And yet they said, "Now we can adopt her." (They had been willing to adopt her before her heart was repaired, because they loved her so much, but we had advised them to wait because we were concerned with the high risk of surgery.)

Rachel was discharged two weeks after her surgery. I thought, "What a triumph! What joy! A little child now has a healthy heart! A sick child is well, has a new life and a mother and father who love her and have taken her as their own!"

Rachel is now seven years old and more beautiful than ever. She is bright, happy, curious and fascinated by everything. The last time I saw her I told her that she was destined for something important in her life. I asked her what she wanted to be. She said, "A nurse." I said to her, "Being a nurse is really good, but why not be a doctor or the President?" After several more minutes of conversation I asked her again and she still said that she wanted to become a nurse. I looked at her and stared at her, and finally she said, "Okay, okay, I will be President then!"

These memories are so warm to me, and yet, I suppose, they are just little stories. However, I hope they convey the love and happiness that can be exchanged among human beings. I truly realize the importance of life and the wealth of loving. The little children convey this message with every part of their being.

Now I share Rachel's story told by her adoptive parents…

RACHEL'S PARENTS TELL THEIR DAUGHTER'S STORY

Our experience as parents of a daughter who has had open heart surgery began, and continues, in a most unusual way. Rachel is adopted.

We had two healthy children of our own, Ann (age eleven) and Richard (age eight). During the winter of that year, we decided to take in infant, pre-adoptive children. After obtaining approval from the county as a home for pre-adoptive children, the local hospital sent us our first foster child; a girl, almost naked, only four days old. Our plan was to keep her for six to eight weeks until adoptive parents could be found.

The first pediatric examination revealed nothing out of the ordinary. At the end of the sixth week, one week before prospective adoptive parents were to see the baby for the first time, Judy took the baby for her second examination. Despite receiving a second healthy diagnosis, Judy called the doctor's attention to what she felt were an exceptionally fast pulse and extremely loud heartbeat. Accordingly, the pediatrician conducted a more focused examination and then acknowledged that something was amiss. He then said he had suspicions, but only a more thorough examination in a hospital could confirm these. We telephoned the county case worker to inform her. As a result, the county officials decided to postpone the adoption proceedings, pending results.

We made arrangements for an examination at the hospital, which was then followed by plans for a cardiac catheterization. Meanwhile, something else had been happening to us. Rachel had come as a little stranger but we had discovered in six weeks we had just about exhausted our emotional ability to remain detached from our little darling. By the time the day for catheterization had arrived, there was no emotional difference between how we felt toward Rachel and our own children. We felt she had been our own through natural birth.

The hospital tests and procedures were completed when Rachel was three months old. The diagnosis confirmed our worst suspicions: major surgery was needed and we learned it would be very risky. We were asked by the county to keep Rachel until she was at least a year old, so that her body would be of sufficient size to provide the working area needed by the team of surgeons.

Knowing the uncertainty of this, and with a realization of the total emotional involvement in which our entire family found itself toward Rachel, we laid our cards on the table with the county officials. We told them that we knew we could not get ourselves through the upcoming ordeal without being able to adopt Rachel. We said this fully understanding the county's practice of not allowing foster parents to become adoptive parents without first being removed from the Foster Parents List and then taking a place in the lineup for adopting children.

Previously we had heard derogatory comments about county "bureaucracy." But in this instance, the county officials could not have been more understanding and helpful. They provided us assurance that we would be allowed to keep Rachel. Nonetheless, they wisely advised us that for the sake of our first two children, we should not obligate ourselves to the tremendous financial burden that the surgery and post-operative care would cost. Rachel would continue in the custody of the county for the time being, so that we would be free of that financial commitment. It was agreed that adoption proceedings would be postponed until after the operation, but, at their suggestion, we submitted a letter of intent to adopt. Then we thought: nine months to go for the operation. If something went wrong, how would we know? What should we do? "You'll know, you'll know," were the only consoling words.

At five months of age, Rachel's eating problems began. She experienced constant vomiting. After much consternation and experimentation, Judy learned that liquefied foods, in general, seemed to stay down. But baby food meat products would not. It was a very challenging situation. During one four-week period, to be certain that Rachel was getting enough nourishment, we reverted her diet to baby formula. At Judy's grandmother's suggestion, we tried bread and milk, and Graham crackers and milk. These worked reasonably well.

A few months month later, the situation worsened drastically. Now almost a year old, her temperament changed abruptly. She was irritable, she coughed constantly and the tempo of her vomiting markedly increased. With continued patience and indulgence, Judy fed her much more, in hopes that some of the food would reach her stomach. A couple of weeks later, we brought her in for her scheduled examination.

Rachel's condition was critical. Her heart had become so enlarged from excessive pressure on weak heart tissue that it filled her chest cavity and was pressing against her esophagus. It was no wonder that that she was coughing and vomiting; food could hardly get past this stricture. The doctors decided to keep Rachel in the hospital. They felt surgery was needed very soon, and they started to inquire at various hospitals, to determine which would offer the best chance of success. We always thought the choice would be a hospital in one of the largest cities in the Northeast. But to our surprise and pleasure, the surgical statistics suggested the best choice would be a regional hospital, fairly close to our home.

It seemed so ironic that the heart surgery was scheduled on Valentine's Day! We had been told during Rachel's early months of life that her chances of surviving until she would be physically able to have surgery were only about ten percent. But with her fighting spirit and good medical care, she had been able to make it thus far. Now, in light of the upcoming surgery, her odds had improved: we were quoted a forty-percent chance of survival. We prayed and prayed to God: "Please let her live!"

Finally in the early afternoon we were told that the operation had been a success. We cried! Shortly thereafter, we were allowed to see Rachel in the Intensive Care Unit. We entered the room and were shocked to see our little girl naked and spread like an eagle on an elevated bed. She was tied in that position to avoid any damaging movement. She had a large bandage running along the middle of her chest, covering the surgical wound. She had an assortment of nine tubes or wires protruding from various parts of her anatomy, which were serving as drains, monitors, intravenous feeding conduits, electrical stimuli conduits, etc. This horrific (to us) scene made an indelible impression. In the several years that passed after the surgery, any kind of hurt that Rachel suffered, even a minor one such as a splinter or cut, brought back the ICU image and made us think, "Why should she have any more suffering? The surgery caused her enough hurt to last a lifetime. What can we do to spare her more hurt?" This is why we cringed at the prospect of another future catheterization.

The day after the operation, Fred visited the county office to begin adoption proceedings. It was completed in only a couple of months, largely due to a very kind and understanding judge.

Rachel was in the ICU for about a week and then was transferred to a recuperation room. There, unfortunately, Rachel contracted a cold (presumably from a student nurse who had one), which manifested itself after she had been discharged and gone home. She had to be transported back to the hospital in an ambulance so that oxygen would be available. Her coughing was so bad that both attendants and Judy were afraid she would die before arrival in the hospital. Fortunately Rachel survived, stayed in the hospital for about a week and then went home for good. In the months that followed, her use of supporting drugs was reduced from five to none within two years. Her weight gain and growth were excellent.

Today, at age seven, Rachel displays more energy than any of her peers and often towers above most of her classmates, even though we know her biological mother was quite short.

We have told Rachel about her operation and about her adoption. She seems to have been more adversely affected by the latter than the former. We have observed Rachel at swim time. The "zipper" chest scar, together with the several associated scars, left her chest with ample evidence of major surgery. But we have never seen Rachel express any inhibition or concern about these scars. And neither have we have ever heard another child inquire about the scars. And Rachel insists on wearing a bikini swimming top in imitation of her older sister.

Family friends and acquaintances watching Rachel at play are often quick to observe, "You would never know she ever had any kind of heart problem." Today, Rachel could not be more a part of our family. Our first two children cannot think of her as anything but their sister, and they respect her so much for what she went through! In physical interplay, she gets spanked when she is naughty, gets jostled by Fred as roughly as our other two children, and she wrestles her bigger sister like a tiger. She has as much stamina and fight in her as anyone her age. She is daring, and is growing like the proverbial weed.

Thus, we want to believe that everything is fine. We took Rachel to her pediatric cardiologist for an annual examination recently. He, too, believes she is developing beautifully. He did raise the prospect of another cardiac catheterization sometime in the future to erase any lingering doubts. We understand the rationale and at the same time are hesitant to authorize another procedure that could cause her more risk and more hurt. Our image of the ICU keeps coming back! We know that medicine is not an exact science, and we will have to continue to sort through these issues for a long time...

CHAPTER 19

Transitioning To A Normal Life With Knowledge And Optimism

GRACE TELLS TOMMY'S AND HIS PARENTS' STORY
Tommy, a blue baby, was born with transposition of the great vessel, a condition in which the main blood vessel to the body is exchanged with the main blood vessel to the lung. Consequently, the body receives all the "blue" (low-in-oxygen) blood and the lungs receive all the "red" (rich-in-oxygen) blood. This is the commonest cause of blue babies, and fortunately since the 1960s there has been an effective surgery for repairing this defect. Still, in the times this story was written, during the early newborn period a temporizing procedure was customarily performed, because the risk of repairing the heart completely in the first month of life was very risky.

The temporizing procedure was conducted in the catheterization laboratory. It consisted of the creation of a communication between the two upper chambers of the heart. By means of this communication, the red blood and the blue blood have an opportunity to mix, thereby supplying redder (though still not normal) blood to the body. The procedure was successful and Tommy was discharged to go home. Over the next few months Tommy managed to do fairly well, but maintained a state of severe blueness. We scheduled the surgical repair of his heart when he was a year old.

However, the surgery was postponed because he was admitted to the hospital with a very high fever. His blueness increased as a result of the fever, to the point that I was afraid that he might have a stroke. It is unusual for children to have strokes, but those who are blue have higher incidences. Fortunately, by carefully observing the level of oxygen and the level of red blood cells, we were able to provide appropriate treatments to avoid a stroke. Nonetheless, we advanced the date of Tommy's surgery on account of his severe blueness.

I recall the circumstances surrounding this surgery and the fears and anxieties of all the physicians and nurses who were involved in Tommy's care. All heart operations are taken seriously and treated with great concern. Yet, certain operations produce a higher state of apprehension. At the date of publication of this book, the mortality for the repair of transposition of the great arteries is quite low. However, over thirty years ago, when this story was written, the mortality was much higher. Our fear and anxiety was heightened in Tommy's case because only a couple of months before another child with the same heart defect had died following surgery.

In Tommy's case the surgery went so well that he was sitting up in his little wagon only a few days afterwards. His older sister was allowed to visit him in the Intensive Care Unit and they had a great time together. Tommy's mom snapped a precious picture of the two. It shows Tommy in his little hospital smock, smiling as he looks at his sister with his right arm raised, his index finger and thumb making a V (victory) sign. It is as though he is saying: "I made it."

In all his subsequent visits to the hospital Tommy has been a smiling, happy baby. At age five he required a pacemaker to control his heartbeat, but somehow this difficulty did not change his optimistic attitude. As I remember Tommy throughout his lifetime, it is hard for me to even remember his suffering, for he seemed not to suffer. Even the word "tolerance" would not be appropriate for Tommy, for he lived life as it came to him and seemed in complete harmony with his circumstances, whether they were "slings and arrows" or the fascinations of a new toy. All things flowed easily. It may be frivolous to project into the future. But I know that Tommy is and always will be one of those true, sincere, open and loving human beings who are a blessing to the world. I'm sure he will do important things in his life.

Tommy's mother tells her story…

TOMMY'S MOTHER TELLS HER SON'S STORY
On a Mother's day I received the most precious gift a mother could want. After a quick and easy delivery I gave birth to our son, Tommy. But within minutes,

it was apparent he was in grave danger. His skin had a bluish tinge and he had difficulty breathing. The doctors knew it was either his heart or his lungs, and told me that that if he made it through the night he would be transferred to a major medical center. Tommy did make it through the night, and the following day the new hospital's staff diagnosed him as having a congenital heart defect known as transposition of the great vessels.

Normally, the pulmonary artery is attached to the right ventricle and carries blood to the lungs to receive a fresh supply of oxygen; and the aorta, arising from the left ventricle, sends oxygenated blood to the rest of the body. In transposition, the locations of these two vessels are reversed. Tommy's aorta was attached to the right ventricle, which receives blood that has returned from the body after giving up most of its oxygen to the body tissues. As a result, in Tommy's case, the aorta conveyed to the body poorly oxygenated blood.

Some infants born with this condition survive because of other defects which fortuitously counteract the effects of transposition. In Tommy's case, a procedure had to be conducted to create a hole in the wall between the two atria, in order to allow oxygenated blood to mix with low-oxygen blood before entering the aorta. This hole was created by inserting a catheter through a vein in Tommy's leg and advancing it through this vein until inside the heart. A balloon-type device, not yet inflated, was attached to the end of the catheter. The catheter passed through the small flap in the wall between the atria. Then the balloon was inflated and pulled back forcefully to tear the wall. The objective of this procedure was to buy some time until Tommy was old enough and strong enough for the open-heart surgery.

Unfortunately, less than a couple of months later the hole started to close. We brought Tommy back to the hospital, where another cardiac catheterization was done. The hole was kept open.

Yet another complication was that Tommy developed pneumonia, from which he recovered. These first few months of his life were naturally very trying, but I always had faith in the doctors and nurses who cared for him. Most importantly, I had faith in Tommy. Despite his defect, he seemed strong and had a good size. I believe he amazed everyone by his steady growth. One thing in particular I had worried about in his early life was the effect that this transposition might have on Tommy's brain. But I was reassured to know that even when the oxygen content of the blood is somewhat lowered, the brain is able to get the oxygen it needs.

Tommy continued to grow and develop. He started smiling at four weeks, lifted his head at three months, sat up at eight months, crawled at eleven months and walked at fourteen months. The only medication he took was Digoxin, to regulate his heart. On the other hand, Tommy tired more easily than a normal child, and turned blue when he cried. Despite this, he started talking at twelve months, seemingly nonstop!

We brought him to the hospital about once a month for checkups, normally an electrocardiogram (EKG) and an X-ray. Tommy was so active that the EKG technician often had difficulty persuading him to lie quiet for the test. Happy but stubborn, nothing could slow him down! The doctors didn't limit his activity (how can one restrict a one-year old child anyway?) because a sick child tends to stop active play of his own accord before becoming overtired.

The corrective surgery was tentatively set for when Tommy would reach three years. But the date was gradually advanced because of his deteriorating condition. It was rescheduled for when he would reach two years of age. The surgical procedure to be performed was the so-called mustard operation. In it, a baffle—a patch of pericardium—would be put in Tommy's heart to reroute the blood.

Finally, the big day! Tommy was in the Operating Room for about six hours. During the procedure he was hooked to the heart-lung machine. Tommy came through the surgery with flying colors and in the afternoon I was allowed into the Intensive Care Unit to see him. The surgeon said to me quite seriously, "Did you see his toes yet?" Worried that something had happened to his feet, I picked up the blanket and saw ten beautiful pink toes! Within a week he was out of the ICU. A few days later his stitches were taken out and on the following day he was discharged to go home.

Tommy was, and still is, very proud of his scars—a badge of courage. He continued to visit the hospital for checkups, but otherwise lived a normal active life. Over a year after his surgery the doctors worried that Tommy might have a leak in his "patch," but fortunately a catheterization showed no leak; his patch had just puckered. Then before starting Kindergarten his EKG showed extra heartbeats, and this required a special EKG a few months later. However, during this time he participated in all school activities and became a member of the swim-gym program at another institution.

A year later we went back to the hospital for a special test. The doctors placed electrodes in Tommy's chest and the monitor was attached to a belt around his waist. He had to wear these devices for 24 hours. But he was not fazed! He thought it was great to be "bionic"! I ran around behind him to make sure his wires were attached and that he didn't take his belt off! This monitoring showed a very slow heart rate, particularly when asleep. His rate fluctuated from slow to very fast, but it was the slow rate that worried the doctors. They had seen this slow rate develop in other children who had had surgical correction of transposition, especially after they had been followed for a few years. They worried that the slow heartbeat could predispose Tommy to an erratic heartbeat, which would be dangerous for him. Their consensus was that Tommy required a pacemaker.

Tommy was admitted to the hospital for the procedure. The surgeon explained to Tommy and to me that the pacemaker carried a lithium-type battery which would last for five to seven years before needing to be recharged. The next day the surgeon inserted the pacemaker in an operation that lasted about two hours. Later that day I visited him in the ICU. He was angry because he had an oxygen mask on and couldn't suck his thumb. Within four days he was out of the ICU, and soon running up and down the hall, usually with a nurse's stethoscope around his neck. In a week he was home playing with his friends and riding his bike. Swimming was the only activity he had to give up during his short convalescence.

The pacemaker heart rate was kept at 65 beats per minute. When Tommy is asleep and his heart rate goes below this number, the pacemaker stimulates his heart to produce the desired rate. There is a bulge on Tommy's chest, but this bulge will appear relatively smaller as he gets bigger and his muscles develop. It doesn't bother him at all, as it might other children. I think it's because he understands so much of what has happened to him.

Tommy is now in first grade, enjoying his school activities and gym classes. He will be starting his gym and swimming classes at another facility. He plans to take his copy of his chest X-ray into school for "show and tell," to explain to classmates what he has gone through.

Tommy will probably have to have this pacemaker for the rest of his life, unless medical technology discovers something new. But even so, I don't think the pacemaker will bother Tommy. It would take a lot more than that to slow Tommy or dampen his zest for life.

The most important advice I could give another parent whose child has a heart defect, or any other major illness, would be to "level" with the child as much as possible. Tell the child in simple terms what is going to be done and why. A child understands and accepts facts more often than adults give him credit for. Instill knowledge...not fear!

PART V
CONCLUSION

CHAPTER 20

A Reflection

There are certain patterns which emerge from the accounts of the parents of my patients, as well as from my own experience.

First, most parents have said that they had become sufficiently acquainted with the technical and scientific aspects. It appears that the mechanical facets of surgeries and procedures had been sufficiently described to them. Most had been given diagrams or study aids to help them understand the nature of their child's heart defect and the type of surgery necessary to repair it. They seemed to be well aware of the possible complications of surgery, as well as the associated death rates. Most said they were well informed of the post-operative equipment that would surround their child. Certainly these were helpful preparations.

On the other hand, a thread that is woven throughout is the insufficient appreciation by medical professionals of the psychological needs of child and parent. It seems that we, the medical professionals, stress communication about the technical and scientific approach. Yet, what I have heard and observed is a sense of loneliness, a separation which is conveyed by a child and sensed, most acutely, by the parent. For instance, we professionals tell the child that we will circumvent the use of needles (of which they are scared) by a small tube that will be placed in the arm; that all medicines will be fed through it, and that he will not feel any pain during surgery. But it seems we do not spend enough time in understanding and allaying the child's fears of separation from, and abandonment by, his parents.

Fortunately many medical centers have liberalized their strict visitation rules in recent years, and allow parents to accompany their child to the pre-operating room. They are not separated until the anesthesiologist is ready to put their child to sleep. I am sure that this accommodation greatly comforts children. Also, nearly all medical centers allow parents to see their child immediately after the surgery, upon his arrival in the Intensive Care Unit. Usually the child is markedly sedated, so he may be only marginally aware of the parents' presence. It is customary to keep the child heavily sedated during this early post-operative period, and I imagine that there is little awareness during this time, but every bit of awareness helps. Perhaps the most valuable time for communication will be on the following day, when the child is awakening and some of the tubes are removed. Liberal visiting hours are most helpful at this stage.

With the rapid advances in medical science, more and more surgeries and procedures are successful, allowing more and more children to get a better appreciation of all that life has to offer, and allowing them to fulfill their dreams. However, occasionally there will be heart-wrenching losses. But I believe that even in loss there is an affirmation of life, in terms of the greater community between parents (with some exceptions), with parents of other children, and with all the staff involved in care, from the famous surgeon to the most humble janitor. In my stories, many children have expressed to me the life force that they experienced, by being able to draw a picture just before surgery, and by watching from the hospital a rainfall that revitalizes the earth. I hope that we who experience the loss of a child, even the loss of any loved one, will reflect on the words of these sick children, and will endeavor to live life to the fullest.

EPILOGUE

Grace's Last Thanksgiving Note: A Farewell

Grace and I were married on the eve of Thanksgiving Day. Every year on that holiday we would write each other a note of gratitude for the blessings of having each other.

Grace wrote the attached note on her last Thanksgiving, before her advancing neurological disease claimed her ability to write, and ultimately claimed her life the following summer.

This note exemplifies Grace's admirable capacity to accept misfortune without complaints, and to appreciate and love others without limits. Her closing expression of love forever is one which I and others should remember during trying times, and emulate in our daily living.

Armando I. Perez, Ph.D.

November 2014

Dearest Man,

This is a special day. We celebrate 29 beautiful years of marriage. It has been a very happy time filled with love and joy. Our love appeared so complete from the start and yet throughout the years our love grows every day.

This past year we have been intensely challenged by my serious illness. Throughout this time I have seen the many expressions of your love shown by your constant care and encouragement. You guard me night and day — awakening in the night to help me to the bathroom, supporting me in the shower, getting my meals, pureeing my food, preparing my medications, taking me to the numerous medical appointments, lifting me from the bed and chair, lifting my weak leg and supporting me to climb stairs, making it possible to get to Church in the wheel chair. You never complain of this heavy burden and somehow find the strength and courage to carry on with incredible loving patience. He who knows love knows God because God is love. You are wonderfully made in the true image and likeness of God.

I John 4:16 "God is love and whoever remains in love ~~remains in God love~~ remains in God and God in him."

Further you exemplify the fruit of the Spirit described by St. Paul in Galatians 5:23: "the fruit of the Spirit is love, joy, peace, patience, kindness, goodness, gentleness, trustfulness and self-control..."

Thank you for all the beautiful years and your love. You are a blessing to me and this world.

Love and respect forever,
Grace

ACKNOWLEDGMENTS

I give my special thanks to individuals who provided invaluable encouragement and comments; namely, Dr. Dolores Tamer (retired Pediatric Cardiologist and Grace's esteemed work colleague for so many years), Dr. Josephine Johnson (retired communications department chair at the University of Miami), Penelope Arango (psychologist, former publisher and fellow church parishioner), Lois Biederman (Grace's niece, who encouraged me to write this book after Grace died and helped me so much during Grace's illness), and my brother Carlos A. Perez. My thanks go also to countless others, too numerous to mention here.

Baby Grace held by her middle-aged mother (Rome, NY, 1938)

Grace with her brother Robert (Rome, NY)

Grace (left) with brother Robert during winter (Rome, NY)

Grace at her First Communion (Rome, NY)

Grace placing flower offering in devotion to the Blessed Mother (Rome, NY)

Grace ready for high school prom (Rome, NY)

Grace with her parents at her pre-med graduation from LeMoyne College (Syracuse, NT)

Grace with fellow Pediatric residents (middle row, third from left)

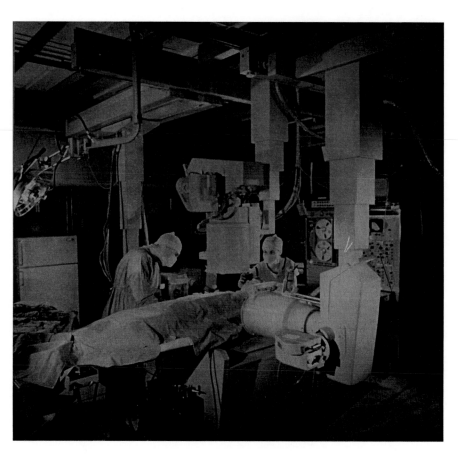

Grace (right) early in her career at cardiac catheterization lab (circa 1970)

Grace taking a break from work (1975)

Grace at her apartment's balcony in Miami, FL (circa 1980)

Grace's and Armando's wedding (Miami Beach, FL, 1985)

Grace and Armando at their wedding reception (Coral Gables, FL, 1985)

Grace ready to greet a young patient (Miami, FL)

Grace with colleague Dr. Dolores Tamer (Miami, FL)

Grace with visiting renowned Dr. Alex Nadas (center),
surrounded by University of Miami faculty members

Grace speaking at a large family gathering (Coral Gables, FL)

Grace and Armando relaxing during a ski vacation (Canada)

Grace and Armando (standing) dining in Madrid, Spain, with Armando's
friends from high school

Grace (right) with Armando's relative Paz at her farm in Asturias, Spain

Grace (far right) with Armando, her relatives, and friend after receiving an
alumna award from LeMoyne College (Syracuse, NY)

Grace with a friend and Armando at their vacation house in the Adirondack
Mountains (Upstate NY)

Grace (far right) at a gathering with Armando's relatives in rural Asturias, Spain

Grace and Armando vacationing at a hotel in Madrid, Spain, where they had spent their honeymoon

Grace (far right) celebrates 40th birthday of longtime heart patient (middle)
(Miami, FL)

Grace in Paris, France (2010)

Grace during terminal illness at home (Coral Gables, FL) accepting award of recognition from Children's Medical Services of State of Florida, surrounded by Armando and medical colleagues (2015)